Praise for the Dating Goddess

The Adventures in Delicious Dating After 40 series of books is based on the blog Adventures in Delicious Dating After 40 at www.DatingGoddess.com. Here are comments from readers.

"The Dating Goddess has put her true voice into this book: smart, funny, truthful. Did I say funny? Yes. In a book on the mysteries of mid-life connections, you couldn't ask for more. A tart and smart companion who tells the ticks, tricks and treasures of dating."

—Dr. Clarissa Pinkola Estes, bestselling author, *Women Who Run With the Wolves: Myths and Stories of the Wild Woman Archetype*

"At last, a dating writer who addresses requirements. You are SO right on! I'm thrilled to have found you!" —Rachel Sarah, author, *Single Mom Seeking*

- "Adventures in Delicious Dating After 40 is a wonderful composite of both the mechanics of post-40 online dating and what the practice of honoring one's self actually looks like. How marvelous your writing is to read. I spent about 2 hours reading and was riveted the whole time." —Maggie Hanna

- "Powerfully heartfelt and honest writing. You are inspiring." —Kare Anderson, Emmy Award winning writer

- "I just love your writing. It is very fresh and gives the reader something to think about." —Kelly Lantz, President & Manager, 55-Alive.com

- "Dating Goddess, you are like a, a, a, well, a goddess to me. You've helped guide me successfully through my re-entry into the dating world after 14 years. I'm an eager student and fast study, and do get myself into situations that others don't know how to deal with -such as 3 dates in one day -— so thankfully you are there! You're the greatest, thanks for all you do for us!" —Jae G.

- "I find your point of view much more interesting than other dating writers. Thanks for always reminding me to enjoy dating life no matter what it throws at you." —Sandy

Date *or* Wait

Are you ready for Mr. Great?

Dating Goddess™

Date or Wait: Are You Ready for Mr. Great?

Second Edition

Cover design by Dave Innis, www.innisanimation.com

Book design by Just Your Type.biz

Internal illustrations by Kimb Tiboni Manson, www.senjula.com

Printed in the United States of America.

ISBN Print: 978-1-930039-33-9

eBook: 978-1-930039-11-7

How to order:

The *Adventures in Delicious Daing After 40* books may be ordered directly from www.DatingGoddess.com

Quantity discounts are also available. Visit us online for updates and additional articles.

The Adventures in Delicious Dating After 40 books are dedicated to my ex-husband since he unexpectedly released me to explore the untethered life of a single woman. I then had the freedom for the experiences, lessons and insights shared in these pages.

Books by Dating Goddess

- *Date or Wait: Are You Ready for Mr. Great?*
- *Assessing Your Assets: Why You're A Great Catch*
- *In Search of King Charming: Who Do I Want to Share My Throne?*
- *Embracing Midlife Men: Insights Into Curious Behaviors*
- *Dipping Your Toe in the Dating Pool: Dive In Without Belly Flopping*
- *Winning at the Online Dating Game: Stack the Deck in Your Favor*
- *Check Him Out Before Going Out: Avoiding Dud Dates*
- *First-Rate First Dates: Increasing the Chances of a Second Date*
- *Real Deal or Faux Beau: Should You Keep Seeing Him?*
- *Multidating Responsibly: Play the Field Without Being A Player*
- *Moving On Gracefully: Break Up Without Heartache*
- *From Fear to Frolic: Get Naked Without Getting Embarrassed*
- *Ironing Out Dating Wrinkles: Work Through Challenges Without Getting Steamed*

Contents

Foreword

The Dating Goddess has provided a rare gem in *Date or Wait*. She offers fresh ideas on a topic that has been around as long as people have been seeking love. She blends her practical ideas, thoughtful insights and playful humor to make *Date or Wait* a fun, thought provoking read.

Her unique perspective on midlife dating – seeing the search for your next love match as an adventure – is a refreshing departure from the typical "here's how to manipulate a man into proposing" book. She shares how you can see nearly every encounter with a prospective suitor as an opportunity to learn something about yourself or men. Dating becomes an exciting classroom, with the Dating Goddess as a fun, engaging, and encouraging teacher, and your dates providing the "lab" to try out new behaviors in attracting the right man. The learning keeps the journey interesting.

The Dating Goddess believes that by looking for the "treasures" in the men you meet you will see hidden gifts that others have missed when only looking at their superficial trappings. You may have to look to find these attributes in some men, as they may be deep inside a less-than-inviting package. At midlife, not everyone looks as handsome, hunky and alluring as when in their twenties or thirties. But beneath a receding hairline or a few extra pounds can be an interesting, loving, adoring — and even sexy — man!

When you apply Dating Goddess's ideas you'll have a lot more fun, meet more interesting men, and be able to apply her philosophy of seeing life as a glass 7/8 full.

Not that every dating experience is rosy. In midlife, we bring some baggage, whether we admit it or not. While confident in some aspects of life, we also have insecurities, perhaps wounds left by past loves, that make us vulnerable. The Dating Goddess discusses how to deal with setbacks as learning opportunities.

This book is not theoretical, written by someone who hasn't dated in 30 years. Instead, the Dating Goddess shares her experiences from the front line, having dated 91 men in 3.5 years after her 20-year marriage dissolved. Her quest for her next mate motivated her to date as many men as possible who met her qualifications. She embraced the concept of being aggressively single. She shares her lessons so you can learn from her epiphanies.

For over two decades, I've known the professional woman who wrote this book. Her friends dubbed her the Dating Goddess after hearing she had 7 dates with 6 men in 5 days. The name is descriptive of a woman who's dated scores of men and still has a positive attitude rather than feeling bitter and jaded.

Why is this book different than other dating books? First, it's focused on the decidedly different experiences midlife dating women face from those in their twenties or thirties. While some things about dating never change, dating after 40 has both advantages and disadvantages.

Secondly, the philosophies embedded in each chapter are applicable to other areas of your life — interacting with your workmates, kids, friends, and in approaching life with verve. The Dating Goddess's approach of learning from every experience — giving people grace, noticing how you feel in a situation, cleaning up misunderstandings, treating others respectfully even if they haven't treated you that way, and many others — allow you to have deeper and more meaningful encounters in life.

Don't delay having your first "date" with the Dating Goddess

So don't delay having your first "date" with the Dating Goddess. I promise that you'll want more and more of this gifted writer's work.

Susan Page

Author of *If I'm So Wonderful, Why Am I Still Single?*

Introduction

This book is designed for anyone who is interested in stories, advice, and lessons from the midlife dating front. If you are over 40 and haven't dated in a while — or even if you have — you'll learn ways to approach dating with zeal, optimism, and hope. Even if you've had more than your share of negative experiences, I'll share how to glean lessons from those adventures, rather than just declaring that "all men are jerks" or "men are just looking for sex."

While most of the perspective is from a woman to women, men's comments, experiences, and lessons have been integrated as appropriate.

This book began as daily entries into my blog, Adventures in Delicious Dating After 40, which has been featured in the *Wall Street Journal* as well as on radio and TV. I wrote about my epiphanies from my and my friends' dating life. The best postings were culled to make this and subsequent books.

This book focuses on the elements to be considered before you actually start dating full bore. But even if you've reentered the dating world, this will give you a foundation of attitude and philosophy to make your adventure more fulfilling.

This book consists of three types of perspectives:

> ***Lessons:*** These are specific experiences I thought would be useful to you. A few lines from my experience illustrate the points.
>
> ***Insights:*** These usually start with an experience I've encountered, then the insights that experience spawned. It is usually comprised of around half story and half insight.
>
> ***Stories:*** These are examples of situations I've experienced — or was currently experiencing when I wrote that piece — that I thought would be entertaining. Or I thought the story would help you see what kind of things happen in the midlife dating world so you'd know what has happened to others.

Because these writings were real time, as they occured, they are often set in the present tense. But they are not chronological. So a reference to "my current beau" may now be many sweethearts ago. I hope this isn't confusing.

I'd love ot hear your stories and questions. Please email them to me at Goddess@DatingGoddess.com. They may make it into the blog or my next book!

Who is the Dating Goddess?

I am a middle-aged, white, professional woman. My husband of nearly 20 years left me in April 2003 when I was 47, 11 days shy of 48. After giving my heart time to heal from the surprise divorce sprung by the man I thought was my soulmate, I started dating 18 months later. Generally, I have had a great time meeting interesting men, some of whom became romantic beaus, some became treasured friends, and some I never heard from again.

I am not a well-preserved, gorgeous, marathon-running middle-aged women

In the beginning, I had dates with single male colleagues, but I quickly found Internet dating was the way to explore the most "inventory" and qualify men who I thought might be a good match.

I am not one of those well-preserved, gorgeous, marathon-running middle-aged women. I have been told I am attractive, but I am overweight and not a gym rat. So while I am active, I do not match the description 90% of men's profiles say they want: slender, athletic, toned, fit. I have some wrinkles — what one sweet suitor mistakenly called dimples. I have what Bridget Jones called "wobbly bits," as most non-surgically enhanced middle-aged women do. My genes — and a lifetime addiction to chocolate — have made their mark. Yet I've met and dated some wonderful men, so even if you're not a lingerie model, you can find guys who will think you're attractive, perhaps even hot!

In my professional life, I am a bestselling author of workplace effectiveness books, professional speaker and management consultant. I've appeared on Oprah, 60 Minutes, and National Public Radio and in the *Wall Street Journa*l and *USA Today*.

This book is intended to not only be useful to others and cathartic for me, but is also the genesis of a new topic for fun, thought-provoking speeches. I'm calling myself a dating philosopher and giving date-a-vational speeches! Let me know if you know a group who would like an entertaining after-lunch speech on how lessons learned from dating have implications in business and personal relationships and well as life philosophies.

How did I come by the Dating Goddess moniker? After a few months of dating dozens of men — one week yielded 7 dates with 6 guys in 5 days — my friends dubbed me this name. I liked it, so it stuck.

I'm purposefully not sharing my picture as I don't want you to think either, "How did she get any dates at all?" or the opposite, "Of course she found it easy to get 91 men to ask her out." I am not hideous (usually) nor am I stunning (without professional hair, makeup and Photoshop!). Some men find me attractive, some don't.

I continue to search for my "one," but I have learned a lot along the way, and my single and not-single friends have loudly encouraged me to share my experiences and lessons in the hopes of helping others navigate the adventure of dating with more success. And to have a delicious time doing it!

Make sure to download your free eBook, Attract Your Next Great Mate: Dating Advice From Top Relationship Experts, *at www.DatingGoddess.com/freebie*

Fresh start. New beginning.

Within a few weeks of my ex announcing he was leaving, these four words — "Fresh start. New beginning." came to me while I was sleeping. I want to say they were in a dream, but they were so vivid and clear it was as if they were said by someone standing next to my bed.

While I was still in deep grief over the dissolution of my marriage, they gave me a perspective — even hope — that all would be fine once it was over.

Today, 4.5 years after my hearing them, they take on new meaning. Perhaps this year will be one of fresh starts and new beginnings for you, starting now.

So what fresh start and new beginning will commence for you today? What would you like to start anew in the relationship realm?

From hurt to flirt

When my husband of 20 years left, I was stunned. I didn't see it coming. After crying in a fetal position for a week, I had a talk with myself. I decided I was going to see if I could turn the situation into something positive. I had been able to do so in other situations, but none quite as debilitating as this one. I decided to see if I could find the "gift" in this life-changing surprise.

He released me to explore the un-tethered life as a single woman

I asked myself, "What could be the opposite of 'my life is over'?" How about, "He has released me to explore the untethered life as a single woman"? It took me a month to say this mantra out loud without laughing.

At first the thought terrified me of re-entering the dating scene middle-aged and overweight. Who would possibly think I was attractive enough to date? Didn't men my age want young, vivacious women with pert, taut, supple bodies? But I began chanting my mantra daily. And I began to date. In earnest. I began flirting with men of all shapes, sizes, and ages — straight, gay, married, single. It was fun!

Soon men initiated flirting with me. I became more playful and had a lot of fun. I began to see I could be attractive — at least attractive enough to entice someone to flirt with me. I began having the life of my mantra — I was living the untethered life as a single woman — and having a blast doing it.

What are you saying to yourself about dating? For example, are you saying "The only men I meet are losers"? Or "All the good men are gay or married"? Or "I'll never find my soul mate"?

How can you change your words to be inspiring? For example, "The men I meet are extraordinary, successful, kind, and caring." "There are abundant good, straight men longing to meet a good woman like me." "My soul mate is just around the corner and is looking for me as hard as I'm looking for him." The more you chant your mantra, the more quickly it will come true!

What will your mantra be?

Dating is like Baskin-Robbins

I compare my philosophy of dating to visiting Baskin-Robbins where I ordered vanilla for 20 years. (Maybe it was Rocky Road at the end!). While I enjoyed vanilla, I want to try new flavors. And I didn't want to jump from vanilla and make a commitment to strawberry without having tasted a little pistachio, chocolate, mint chip, and more.

So I made a list of men I'd like to "try" (just like I "try" ice cream flavors). I got out my little pink tasting spoon.

I like smart men, so I wanted to try a lawyer, doctor, CEO, and venture capitalist. I like large men, so I wanted to try an ex-pro football player and ex-pro basketball player. I love men with accents, so I wanted to try some who came from abroad. You get the picture. I landed dates with all of the above and many more.

In the beginning I even gave my guys ice cream flavor names. Butter Pecan for the Ph.D. in electrical engineering because he was interesting and refined.

Double Dip Chocolate with Nuts for the fun-loving, 6-foot-9, black former pro-basketball player. Bubblegum for the 32-year-old boy toy. Jamoca Almond Fudge for the Caribbean-born gentleman. Cafe Olé for the Brazilian salsa dancer. Passionfruit for the good kisser. Chunky Monkey for the chubby one. Hunka Burnin' Fudge — well, you can guess that one was eye candy!

But I quickly ran out of nicknames, as I had more guys than Baskin-Robbins had flavors. Even borrowing from Ben and Jerry, I was burning through flavors faster than a double dip on a sweltering August day.

So I encourage you to try dates with men you might have turned away if you'd strictly adhered to your list of desired traits. Some of my favorite treasures have come from going out with men who wouldn't have been on my radar screen before. (A 6-foot-9 guy? "No way," I used to think. But Double Dip Chocolate with Nuts has become one of my dearest pals.)

So don't limit your choices of flavors too much. Yes, those you date need to have the same values as you. But who cares if a man who lists himself as "athletic" in his profile is 40 pounds overweight? Extra weight can be shed, but integrity, intellect, thoughtfulness, respect, and caring are embedded. You can't change that.

What are the ingredients for the flavors of men you want to try?

You've got to kiss a lot of...princes!

Most of the women over 40 I talk to feel frustrated about dating because they think many men are cads, players, jerks — in other words, frogs!

I'm here to jump in with another view.

In my first 3.5 years of dating, I went out with 91 men. No, that's not 91 dates, but 91 individual men. Many multiple times. I've had a few 6- to 12-week relationships and one 6-month beau.

Out of all those men, I've had 9 bad first dates. That's 10% — not bad, really. On the positive side, I've met a number of interesting, kind, generous gentlemen. Those are the princes, although none of them became my long-term prince. There was some fatal flaw that I — or they — deemed to be a deal breaker. Am I being overly picky? Perhaps. But after realizing I'd "settled" in my marriage of 20 years, I don't want to do that to my next partner — or me — again.

Please know that if you've had a bad encounter or two, it doesn't mean everyone out there fits the definition of cad, loser or jerk. It just means you have to do a better job screening by email and phone before you go on a date. You can tell a lot about others by the questions they ask — or don't ask — and what they tell you. I've saved myself many hours of suffering through a bad date by not saying "yes" to an invitation from someone who interrupted me constantly, was arrogant, filthy-mouthed, or sex-focused.

A dozen or more of my gems still keep in contact, even though we decided we weren't good matches. We still enjoy each other's company. I see them as princes for someone else. And I get to enjoy their "princeness" without the complications and expectations of becoming a couple. Besides, they're great resources when I want to ask my "Why would a guy..." questions.

You'll find princes everywhere. Give a guy a chance to see if he is your prince. I know my prince is looking for me as hard as I'm looking for him. But if I don't even answer his emails, how will I ever know?

What's your definition of dating success?

For many women the answer to this question would be, "To find my next love/husband/mate." I invite you to consider another possible definition.

If someone were to ask you, "What is your definition of success in life?" you would probably not answer, "To find my way to death." Both definitions focus on the end result, not the process.

To the second question, you would probably answer something like, "To enjoy myself, laugh, grow, love, make a difference for others and live life fully." You'd focus on enjoying the process, not on the end result. I believe the definition of successful dating needs to include appreciating the adventure.

Not that all aspects of the adventure are thrilling. Think of a trip you've taken to a destination you really wanted to visit. Did you like all parts of your journey to Paris? What about the long plane ride or the taxi trip to your hotel? Most of us wouldn't consider these experiences particularly pleasurable. However, if you engage your seatmate on the plane, catch up on your sleep, and/or read an enthralling book, the journey is pleasurable.

Your trip from the airport can be interesting if you notice the people and architecture and query the cab driver on favorite non-touristy sites. It depends on what you make of the experience. I once had a grand time having a picnic in a Paris laundromat while doing my wash.

Consider defining dating success as something along these lines:

> *"To enjoy meeting and getting to know interesting men, broadening myself through new experiences, feeling the thrill of new romance, being willing to encounter the broad range of emotions from delight and love to disappointment and hurt, growing as a person and becoming more centered in what I want and who I am. And when the time is right, to meet my next long-term love."*

With this definition, you are bound to be successful. And when you do meet your guy, you will be so enticing he won't ever want to let you go.

Are you open to receiving?

Do you think of yourself as feminine? When I hear that word, I think of the terms usually used to define the word: delicacy, prettiness, sensitivity, gentleness, compassion. I conjure up an image of a demure, eyelash-batting, quiet girl/woman wearing pink lace and crinolines — a la Melanie Hamilton, Scarlet's rival in *Gone With the Wind*. Well, a 21st Century version, of course.

I am nothing like that image or most of those descriptive terms. And yet I know I can be feminine.

When I took the "Making Sense of Men*" evening seminar, I learned a different take on femininity. The author of the program, Alison Armstrong, defines it differently. Her description of femininity is centered around receptivity.

She says (and I'm paraphrasing here) men are drawn to women they can contribute to in some way. That is not to say we need to be damsels in distress. Not at all. We can still be our usual confident, competent, strong selves. But we have to give off vibes that we are willing to receive.

"Receive what?" you aptly ask. "I am financially and emotionally sound. I don't need a man. However, I'd like to have a good, fun, caring man in my life."

Understood. When men like you, whether romantically or as a pal, they offer to help you or be with you. They will offer advice, which some of us interpret as "He must think I'm clueless" and we get upset. A man may also show his fondness of you by warning you ("The weather is turning nasty, so be careful driving on the freeway"), which again infuriates us because we think he must think we're dolts.

Let me give some examples of what some strong, independent women do.

- A man you are interested in asks you out for lunch/dinner. You insist on going Dutch as you don't want there to be any underlying feeling that you owe him anything. Instead, if he offers, let him buy. He likes taking you out. Let him. Instead of arm wrestling him for the bill, smile, say thank you and that you appreciate his generosity. If you feel compelled to even the score, tell him you'd like to treat next time. Or offer to buy after-dinner drinks and/or dessert. Or invite him to your house for dinner next time.
- A guy you've been dating a few times and feel safe with offers to pick you up at your home

for a date, even though it's out of his way. You could insist on meeting him at the venue because it would be easier on him. When you accept his offer, you're allowing him to do something nice for you. Men like this.

- A male pal offers to walk you to your car/the subway/the bus stop on a dark, blustery night. You say, "Thanks, but I'm fine." He's showing he cares for you by wanting to ensure your safety and spend a little more time with you. Let him. Say thank you.

- You are struggling with some boxes. A neighbor (not a sleazeball) offers to help. You decline because you don't want to put him out. Let him help. He wouldn't have offered if he wasn't fine with doing it. It will make him feel better about himself to have helped.

You show your openness and receptivity in many simple ways. If a man you like and feel safe with offers something that would be helpful or nice, accept. And verbalize your appreciation afterwards. That's what they want — to be noticed and thanked. If a man likes you, he wants to make you happy and give you what you want — even if there are no romantic implications.

For example, after I gave a presentation recently, a new colleague/friend in the audience told me he was so inspired that he was now committed to taking action within 48 hours. I offered to be his accountability partner. He accepted. I threw out this consequence if he didn't accomplish what he promised: he'd send me a pound of Godiva. He laughed. "What flavor?" "Milk chocolate. With nuts. But if you're really committed, it doesn't matter because you won't be sending it." We laughed.

He accomplished what he promised within the time frame and emailed me proof. The next day a box of chocolates arrived, not because he missed his deadline, which he hadn't, but because he said he appreciated my support. And I was glad I'd said what I wanted and he listened! In the past I just would have said, "Email me when it's accomplished." Or after the Godiva exchange, said "No, really, you don't have to do anything." But he shared that it gave him much pleasure to surprise me with this, even though he'd met his part of the bargain. And I thanked him.

I don't see this receiving business being against any feminist principles any of us might hold. Nor do I see that receiving nice behaviors means you have to return them, but you could if you wanted. You're not demanding, you're simply receiving. And if he wants to know more about how to make you happy, you'll share.

Do you find yourself not allowing men to do things for you? If so, why? Are you concerned it will imply you owe him something back? Can you let go and just receive? And appreciate him for his kindness?

* *For more information on this program, go to www.understandmen.com*

Dating: A self-designed personal-growth workshop

Maybe you're like me and have attended a lot of seminars. Perhaps some of these have been personal-growth workshops. After taking a bunch of them, you realize you can design a lot of the activities yourself. If you are a good student, you see that you don't really need someone else to design the processes and lead you through them. You can do this for yourself.

You become adept at making many life events learning experiences. Sometimes they are unpleasant episodes, but even those can produce valuable lessons.

Thus it is with dating. No matter what happens, there's a lesson for you. It could be affirming: "Great decision. Do that again." Or it could be admonishing: "That was dumb. How could you let yourself get in that situation?" Either way, you've added to your wisdom arsenal, even if it was just reinforcing information you already knew.

Once you appreciate all the lessons you get from an experience after the fact, you become more emboldened to be proactive about gaining the lessons. You plan activities that will force you to examine your feelings and behaviors. "Like what?" you ask.

Let's say in the past you've allowed intimacy to just unfold spontaneously, without thinking beforehand, "Do I want to have sex with this guy? If I do have sex with him, what will be my expectations of him afterward? I usually then become more attached to a guy, so will I be clingy? Or hurt if he doesn't call the next day or act like we're an item now?" One thing has always led to another, sometimes with the help of alcohol or loneliness or skin hunger. And afterward, if he didn't call or step up his contact with you, you felt slutty, or used, or hurt.

No matter what happens, there is a lesson for you.

So how could you be proactive about designing a process that would cause you to have a new lesson in this example? What if you decided you would talk to the guy you are dating about sex before you get too far into the activities to want to stop? What if after some extended smooching, you paused and said, "Can we talk about sex?" It's not too early in the relationship to do so, and it appears he's interested in you romantically.

But your clothes (at least most of them) are still on, so you're not at a place where you are promising something that you may not deliver.

The lesson for you would be that you learned you could have a serious discussion with the man you're dating. If he poo-poos talking about it, gets upset that you've stopped the action, or gives you one-word responses while trying to remove your clothes, you know all you need about this man to not continue. If he's able to stop and have a discussion about what sex means to each of you, what you need from him to have sex with him eventually (not tonight), and about STDs/safe sex/ protection, you see that you are with someone who is emotionally mature.

But if the discussion is difficult for you to bring up, you then get to examine why. Is it that you are afraid of being rejected for stopping the action? He might get annoyed and leave, never to call again? What is it in you that finds this discussion so difficult that you've never brought it up with anyone before?

So no matter what happens, you get a chance to examine your thoughts and feelings which led to the actions. And you also get to examine how you felt about yourself afterwards. All of which makes for a very rich personal-growth seminar!

How have you found dating to be a personal-growth experience? What questions have you learned to ask yourself that squeeze learnings out of nearly every dating experience?

Hands-on dating research

Yesterday an author friend shared that she was doing hands-on research for a book by remodeling her own house. I thought,

"I'm doing 'hands-on' research myself — on dating!" Of course, sometimes the hands-on part is welcomed — sometimes not. ☺

But what am I really researching?

Sometimes the hands-on part is welcomed — sometimes not.

First, I am researching what I want and don't want in a man and a relationship. While you would think that you would be pretty clear about this, the truth is it takes some experimentation to really know. You have to be around different potential suitors to see what fits and what doesn't.

Second, I am researching what makes men click.

What works with them and what doesn't? While men can be simple creatures, if you don't fully understand what can go on in their heads, you will be frustrated.

Sometimes the research can be fun. Other times it can be tiresome or even, although thankfully rare, painful. But with each experience you add to your research base and refine your skills. A researcher knows not every experiment will be a success, but she learns from each one. So you add to your knowledge base with each experience.

Have you been researching? If so, what have you learned? If not, get out there and start collecting date-a.

Being present to the presents

My newly divorced 48-year-old neighbor asked how to continue to be positive and upbeat after going out with lots of men without finding "The One."

I told her my philosophy is "never a wasted evening." In my dating journey, I've met some wonderful men and had some great times, lots of laughter, and some memorable activities. I've experienced some close connections. I reawakened some feelings I thought were buried from the painful divorce. I've learned a lot about myself and about men.

And even the less-than-stellar dates — and the very few bad dates — had a lesson attached. From one, "Signs he won't be asking for a second date"* was spawned. Even "Date was a losing bet"* birthed a funny story which amuses my friends and was a good lesson for me and others. Many first dates end in ambivalence, thus a piece called "Ambivalence"*. And I've learned to spot deal breakers quickly so wrote "First-date red flags that this guy isn't for you"*.

My friend pointed out that these lessons took approaching the date with consciousness. They weren't merely funny stories bashing men and labeling the guy a loser. (I don't use that term, even with the guy who dumped me after 10 minutes [this story is in the *First-Rate First Dates: Increase the Chance of a Second Date*], or with others who exhibited uncouth behaviors.)

She observed it takes a shift of focus to be present during the date to notice what's happening, your feelings about it, and analyze what is or isn't working. This is what psychologists call a "participant observer" perspective. It's the ability to take note of what's going on with and around you while you're in the activity, then articulate and analyze it afterward, melding subjectivity with objectivity. You can do it if you work at being able to be present to what's being said as well as how you are reacting to it.

To me, this is a key to dating positively. Dating is a vehicle to explore what you want and don't want, what you do that makes a date a success or not, what a man does or doesn't do that draws you to him or pushes you away. Without the presence to see the lessons, you just walk away feeling, "I like him" or not. There is no discernment about what you like or don't, so no way to look for the traits you like in a future guy, or avoid what you don't like.

Look for the gifts — the presents — in all your encounters during the dating process. Starting with the first contact, emails, phone calls, face-to-face meetings, touching, kissing, etc., just notice how you feel and what's going on. You may want to log what works for you and what doesn't and add these items to your boyfriend job description (in the *In Search of King Charming* book).

* These pieces are all in the *First-Rate First Dates: Increase the Chance of a Second Date* book.

Dating is like a box of chocolates

With apologies to Forrest Gump's momma (and author Winston Groom), dating is like a box of chocolates.

I've written about how dating is like Baskin-Robbins (page 5) and house hunting (page 47).

But it struck me recently — while nibbling on a box of chocolates — how similar the two can be. And was Momma (Winston) ever so right — you never know what you're gonna get.

See if you agree with my comparisons.

- I love receiving a box of chocolate, whether Godiva, Ethel M, See's, Russell Stover, or a boutique brand. But the box sets the tone. Godiva and other top brands realize the importance of their packaging. I am drawn to a man who is packaged (dresses) well, too.
- I want my favorites first, whether chocolate or men. If you receive several invitations for an

evening or weekend, say "yes" to your favorite guy, begging off with the other(s), saving them for another day.

- I don't like to share good chocolates — or good men. When I find something/someone delectable, I don't want to share. Call me selfish, but I want it/him all to myself.

- Sometimes, but rarely, I overdose on too much of a good thing. If I gorge on scrumptious chocolate, I get a tummy ache. Sometimes if you indulge by spending a lot of time with a yummy guy, his foibles surface and he's less desirable. Best to ration your time together so it's always delicious.

You never know what you're gonna get

- Expensive chocolate can be heavenly. But so can Hershey's or Dove. Men don't have to be rich to be appreciated. But rich men, like expensive chocolate, often come in more enticing wrappings.

- What happens when you get to the dregs — the pieces you're not that fond of? With chocolates, I salvage as much as I can, usually gnawing the chocolate coating around a center I don't like. There is always something salvageable. While rarely has a date gone sour, some have been at the far end of the desirable scale. But there is always a lesson for you, even with dates that end less than deliciously.

When the box is empty, I am sad but know my favorites are abundantly available with a mouse click. I can order more whenever the whim hits. When your dating pipeline has thinned, log onto your online dating site and shop for a new favorite or two.

Why do we date?

Common responses to this question include: to have fun, romance, companionship, a family, sex, a "soft place to land," affection, love, excitement, security, marriage, a life partner, to love and be loved, and eliminate loneliness. All good reasons.

However, I think one of the most profound reasons is stated by Susan Sarandon's character Beverly Clark, in the American version of the movie *Shall We Dance.* When asked why people marry, Beverly says, "We need a witness to our lives. There are a billion people on the planet. I mean, what does any one life really mean? But in a marriage, you're promising to care about everything. The good things, the bad things, the terrible things, the mundane things … all of it, all of the time, every day. You're saying, 'Your life will not go unnoticed because I will notice it. Your life will not go unwitnessed because I will be your witness.'"

While not commonly acknowledged, I think this core "witnessing" is important. What it says to me is that we want someone who cares about us long term. Yes, we have family and friends, but we yearn for a daily confidant, someone with whom to share our everyday triumphs, setbacks, and adventures. Yes, we could do that with a close family member or friend, but when you share it with someone you are hoping to build a life with, it takes on a deeper significance.

I understand that not all people want or expect their sweetie to be their best friend. They don't intend to tell that person their deepest secrets, as some of those may be about yearnings or fantasies of another person. It's usually best to leave those for sharing with a best friend with whom you're not sleeping. However, most people say they want their lover to be at least their friend, and often their best friend. They want someone to "witness" their lives.

A man I was seeing called me every day to tell me about his day and ask about mine. While I find it more interesting to talk about deeper topics, he often called on a break or when he couldn't talk long. So the situation didn't lend itself to talking about philosophy, hopes, dreams, fears. However, I understand that he wanted me to be a witness to his life, and he to mine. When we had more extended time together, we talked about more important topics. So I allowed the "reporting in" chats to nurture the witnessing part of our budding relationship.

So, why do you date? What do you think about this concept of "witnessing?"

Make your own rules for dating after 40

After sharing information about my dating life with a married friend, she said she was glad she wasn't dating now because there are no rules. When she was dating (40 years ago) there were rules.

"Like what?" I asked.

"No kissing on the first date."

"Really?" I responded incredulously. "I've had some fantastic kisses on the first date. What else?"

"No sleeping together on the first date."

I agree with that one. "Go on."

"Men are gentlemen and open doors, pay for

> the date, make sure you get home safely." OK, those are fine.
>
> "But there really aren't any rules," I explained. "People come from different experiences, so you have to just be clear on what *your* rules are and don't bend them."

Which can be hard. If you are really into each other, it would be easy to progress as if you'd known each other for a while. "It just feels so comfortable," you tell yourself. However, that momentary comfort will lapse into hurt and betrayal if you allow yourself to go farther than your "rule" would warrant, then he never calls again. You feel used, undisciplined, and perhaps slutty.

So know your own rules and boundaries. And when you want to ignore them — or he is coaxing you to do so — know it's time to end the date for today. I'm all for spontaneity, but know that sometimes spontaneous actions cause a lot of pain later.

Courage and dating

Do you think dating takes courage? I hadn't thought about it that way until in a class I was taking I briefly shared how I'd come to reenter the dating world, and how much I've learned from many of the men I've met. I was surprised when the instructor told me she was awed by the courage it takes to keep at it without having yet met Mr. Right. Afterward, a number of midlife women told me they either hadn't dated since they've found themselves single, or have dated but been frustrated so gave up. They were reenergized at hearing there were lots of great guys around.

I don't think of myself as a particularly courageous person, although I've participated in activities (fire walking, climbing a 25-foot pole then leaping off, swimming with stingrays) that the majority of the population wouldn't consider doing. However, I come up short when I compare myself to mountain climbers, sky divers, race car drivers and others whose courage far outpaces mine.

But I had to agree that dating does take courage. You make yourself vulnerable risking rejection by putting yourself out there, warts, double chins, wrinkles, extra pounds and all. I have been rejected, sometimes painfully, but often when I'm not a match for someone my date either says so matter-of-factly, or, if he has no courage, just disappears.

You have to continuously put yourself in the dating scene if you want to have the highest probability of success. That's why I utilize online dating. The other options to find a mate haven't been very effective for me. You can go about your normal business and hope to run into Mr. Right or be introduced to him by friends. Or you can just stay at home by yourself and be lonely. By putting yourself in the game you hone your flirting, dating, and communication skills (if you're at all conscious), and you clarify what you want and don't want.

So if you haven't yet dipped your toe in the dating water, I encourage you to start wading. The water may be a little bracing at first, but you'll get used to it and you'll find yourself swimming in men in no time!

Facing fear in dating

Recently, I noticed myself feeling a bit nervous before a coffee date to meet a new guy, something I hadn't felt in a while. I wondered if he would be nice or would ditch me within a few minutes. Would there be that wonderful spark I've felt on a few first meetings, or that look of disappointment I've seen a few times?

This uncertainty — this risk taking — is part of what makes dating difficult. The first meetings can be so nerve wracking that they prevent many people from putting their toe in the dating pool.

In my quest for wisdom about courage and taking risks in life, I came upon *I Could Do Anything If I Only Knew What it Was* by Barbara Sher. In it she says:

> *"Most inaction isn't solely because of indecision — it's because of fear. But every time you want to do something that scares you, and you dare to do it, your self-esteem goes up a few degrees. When you're fearful but you step forward anyway, you do yourself a great service. Even if someone slams the door in your face — the worst outcome you can imagine — it doesn't*

> *matter. You're a success every time you face down fear. You can feel that success. You feel elated or determined; either way the feeling is intoxicating.*
>
> *"But every time you let yourself down by not acting, you can feel your self-esteem drop a few degrees. Your morale sinks along with your self-esteem.*
>
> *"What will determine the course of your life more than any other one thing is whether or not you're willing to tolerate necessary discomfort."*

Are you putting off contacting someone you think is attractive? Do you have a phone number for a guy who's invited you to call, but you haven't yet? If so and you need more than Barbara's advice above, read "What would you do if you were brave?" (page 41) and "The first time … calling him" (in the *Check Him Out Before Going Out: Avoiding Dud Dates* book).

When you've done something uncomfortable how did you feel afterward?

Dating requires risk taking

Many women don't want to get back into the dating scene because they know it will require them to take some risks: being rejected, getting a broken heart, being hurt. But without risks in life, rewards are small. If you want to live completely within your comfort zone and not press your limits, you will stay where you are now. If you know you are happier coupled than alone, you may not ever find your special someone without taking some risks.

As long as you are clear on the risks, you can mitigate the chances of something adverse happening, or you can minimize its effect on you if it does. When you take calculated risks — nothing stupid, but pressing your envelope of comfort — you will be amazed at how you grow.

I liken dating to some of the activities I experienced when I led private women's leadership retreats at the spa/resort, Miraval, in Arizona. My ex had just left me a few months earlier, and I used this time to reflect and work on myself, as well as assist others.

One of the Miraval activities included in my curriculum was climbing a 25-foot pole, standing on top, then leaping off. I participated along with my group. We would climb the pole wearing a harness and be belayed by a strong rope with a team of three holding tightly so there was no way you could fall.

Feeling worn out the day of this activity, I didn't really feel like stretching my comfort limits. Stretching out on the massage table was more what I had in mind. The storm clouds were approaching, so I hoped that if I procrastinated long enough, the rains would come and I could bail out. When the leader, Kevin, asked for people to choose their climbing order, I took the last spot.

I watched the younger women scamper up the 25-foot telephone pole in seconds, seemingly leap on top and stand at attention. One woman was so confident, she did a one-legged yoga pose on the dinner-plate-sized disk on top.

Finally, it was my turn. Would I do it or pass? Kevin yelled my number. I paused while I made my decision. I thought, "Drat, I guess I have to participate with my group."

I climbed the pole reasonably easily, considering my lack of energy. I guess adrenaline had kicked in. I was okay as long as I didn't look down. Then, at the top, I ran out of rungs to hang onto. The only thing left was to hang onto the disk on the top, which, by the way, rotates!

I grabbed on, which meant I had to hang over the

top so I could balance to get one foot on the disk. Looking straight down 25 feet was unnerving. But I placed one foot on the disk. Now, how to get the other one up? This was hard, as I had to shift my weight onto the top foot and balance while bringing the other foot up. Breathe, focus, OK, now! Did it!

You may never find your special someone without taking some risks

I hung on, folded over with both hands hanging onto the disk and both feet on top of it. Now to stand up — with nothing to hang on to or with which to steady myself. Talk about faith!

I took a deep breath and asked myself,—"What are you willing to take a stand for?" The answer came immediately: "My new life!" I stood up confidently. Yippee! I looked around the beautiful high desert and enjoyed watching the storm clouds against the prominent peaks. Beautiful.

As I prepared to dismount, Kevin asked, "What are you leaping into?" I replied, "I'm leaping into my new life!" With that I turned on the disk — a 9.9-degree of difficulty — and leapt off the pole!

What did I learn?

- Isn't so much of life just putting one foot in front of (or above) the other?

- When you're clear on your goal, you trudge forward, even if you want to give up.
- Take your time if you are scared. Remind yourself of what you need. Breathe, focus.
- When faced with a very difficult task, remind yourself of something that inspires you. It will give you the energy and focus to take a stand.
- You can accomplish amazing things when you are balanced, clear on what you want, focused and grounded.
- With every action, be clear in what you want. I was clear I wanted to leap into my new life with energy, courage, passion and clarity.

See if you can apply these lessons to dating. Yes, it is a risk. But if you want to be coupled again, you have to face your fears. Are you willing to take a stand for finding your love match?

What would you do if you were brave?

At the beginning of our dating adventure, we would be wise to ask ourselves the question above.

The amazing musical artist Jana Stanfield created a song around this question. "If I Were Brave" goes, in part:

What would I do if I knew I could not fail?
If I believed, would the wind always fill up my sail?
How far would I go? What could I achieve,
trusting the hero in me?

What if we're all meant to do what we secretly dream?
What would you ask if you knew you could have anything?
Like the mighty oak sleeps in the heart of a seed,
are there miracles in you and me?
If I refuse to listen to the voice of fear,
would the voice of courage whisper in my ear?

If I were brave, I'd walk the razor's edge,

where fools and dreamers dare to tread.
I'd never lose faith, even when losing my way.
What step would I take today, if I were brave?

What would I do today, if I were brave?

© Jana Stanfield, www.JanaStanfield.com

If I were brave I would…

… attend more functions where there would be men I might find appealing, like professional meetings and singles events.

… make the first move with someone I find attractive, saying "hello" and starting a conversation.

… speak up sooner when something isn't working, even at the risk of losing the guy. If he can't handle it, we aren't a match.

… reconnect with someone I really liked if we parted amicably.

… end every liaison cleanly, whether it's only a coffee date or longer-term connection. Don't allow myself to just disappear, as I hate it when men do this, but instead communicate "it's not a match" with those who I've met for a date.

How would you date differently if you were brave? If you weren't concerned about rejection or getting a bruised heart, but instead led your dating life with the attitude of being aggressively single and thoroughly appreciating the process of finding your next love?

I'm glad dating is hard

I bet you're thinking, "'I'm glad dating is hard' is an odd approach. Why would anyone want dating to be hard?" At first blush, it sounds strange. Let me explain.

The late Art Berg, was one of the best motivational speakers in the world until his death at age 39 in 2002. He wrote several books, was named 1992 Young Entrepreneur of the Year by the Small Business Administration, and Success magazine featured him as one of the Great Comebacks of the Year.

"Come back from what?" you may ask.

In 1983, 21-year-old Art broke his neck in a serious automobile accident, leaving him a quadriplegic. His inspiring story includes his recovery and subsequent ability to become a world-class wheelchair athlete enjoying a variety of sports, including full-contact wheelchair rugby (like those in the movie *Murderball*) and ultra marathon cycling. But that is not what he shared with his audiences.

In his keynote speeches, he talked about his life as a scuba-diving, ATV-riding, RV-driving adventurer, husband and father of two. But one of his most inspiring stories was not told on the lecture circuit. After hearing this, I now apply the lesson to my life, including dating.

When in the hospital recovering from the accident, he had to make decisions that would affect the rest of his life. One of the choices was what kind of wheelchair to use. He could have a motorized one, which the doctors highly recommended because of his limited hand functions, or a hand-powered one. Art insisted on the latter. Why? Because he knew that if he chose the motorized one it would be too easy for him to get complacent — in his words, lazy. He knew the workout the hand-powered chair provided would keep his arms strong, hands flexible and internal organs functioning. A major problem for quadriplegics, he said, was vital body parts atrophied because of lack of exercise.

This is just one example of his mantra —"Be grateful that life is hard." "Hard" in terms of wheelchair power would keep him vigorous, active, healthy and alive a lot longer.

But he went further in living this philosophy. He said that his accident was the best thing that ever happened to him. Why? Because it forced him to face his inner demons, to push himself past what he thought were his limits, to become the man that the Baltimore Ravens adopted as their spiritual good luck charm the year they won the Super Bowl. (He proudly wore the Super Bowl ring they gave to him for being such a key part of their team.)

He told me that he would not have become the man he did, nor would he have accomplished all that he had, if life were not hard. He had to dig for inner strength when he insisted on dressing himself the first time after his accident. It took 4 hours. He was adamant about scuba diving with his family. He even drove his family's RV and piloted their motor boat. He took his family on cruises and played with them on the beach. Very little slowed this man down. You or I might have seen roadblocks, but Art said they were just challenges he'd figure a way around.

So what does this have to do with dating? Dating is hard. It requires courage to date. Rejection stings. You have to risk getting your heart — and ego — bruised. You have to be willing to spend an hour getting "dated up" so you look good on a first date, then discover within 10 minutes the guy isn't a good fit. But if you want to live your life to the fullest and find your love match, not letting the setbacks force you to swear off dating, you have to keep going. Going out, that is. Dating.

Art continued living fully after his accident. He didn't give up. He could have and no one would have judged him poorly for it. His life would have been much easier if he chose the motorized wheelchair. But he knew it would be better for him if he took the hard path, not the easy one.

If he had given up, the world would have missed hearing this remarkable man's stories of his life and lessons. He was an exemplar for the rest of us to stop whining about what isn't working in our lives and just live fully — and be appreciative for every part of it, good and bad. He died so early, legions of people won't hear his funny stories and sage wisdom. But hundreds of thousands did hear him in person or on video, and his books are still available from his web site.

So next time you think, "Dating is hard," be grateful. If you are consciously dating, looking for the presents, appreciating the treasures, and noting the lessons you're learning about yourself, you will appreciate that the toughness is making you a stronger, better person. If you begin to get discouraged, think of how Art might approach the situation. He is still a motivator, however, now it's from heaven instead of from stage.

What are you grateful about that is or has been hard?

Dating is like house hunting

"He who hesitates is a damned fool."

—Mae West

My friend Ken Braly wrote a hilarious piece — "Finding A House, Finding A Spouse" (read it at www.DatingGoddess.com) — about how dating is like shopping for a home. Follow me for the metaphor.

If you are shopping for a new home, you would want to see properties that are close to what you're looking for as soon as possible. You have some urgency because you know the property is on the market and many others are looking at the same place. If you don't act quickly, you could miss out on your dream home.

Sometimes I am surprised by the guys who start emailing and/or calling but don't seem to have any urgency about meeting. The only conclusion I can make is they aren't that interested in me. Of course, they may already be dating someone and fishing to have a "reserve" woman in case the current one doesn't work out.

So by not setting something up, they may be missing out on their dream woman. I'm not meaning to sound conceited, as the knife cuts both ways. If I ignore the calls or emails of someone who seems promising, he may become disinterested or meet someone who he thinks better fits his criteria.

If a man seems too urgent — pressing to meet me the same day we connect — then he seems desperate. There has to be a balance.

But if he's made contact, we've emailed and chatted, and there's no "close" for the date, I get the impression he's not very interested. Even if he is traveling the next day, most guys who are interested will put something on their calendar for when they return.

So don't let your potential dream guy move on by not responding within a day or two of his contact. And if he doesn't invite you to meet him within a week of your chatting and emailing, he probably isn't that interested. Move on, as there are other properties to explore!

Read "Finding A House, Finding A Spouse" at DatingGoddess.com

Being aggressively single

Graham Davies describes himself as "aggressively single." He's 47 and has a highly successful speaking business in Europe and the US.

Friends tease me about the number of men I've gone out with in the last 3.5 years. Often they exclaim, "I haven't dated that many people in my life!" Well, they found their sweetie quicker than I have, or they are happy being unattached. Like Graham, right now I'm being aggressively single.

What does that mean exactly? For Graham it means he enjoys dating around. He has a Bond mystique. Women flock to him although he's not classically handsome. He smiles often, flirts easily, is intelligent, funny, quick witted, good mannered and comfortable with himself. Not being GQ beautiful works in his favor — it disarms women's initial response to a traditionally good-looking man: "He must be a player."

What does being aggressively single mean for me? That I'm willing to have coffee with men who meet many of my criteria, which are, believe it or not, pretty high. When people hear the number of men I've gone out with, they naturally assume I will see any man who asks. This is not the case. I turn down all but a small percentage of the requests for a meeting.

Aggressively single means you meet a lot of people who you discover aren't a good fit once you have a face-to-face. You have to be willing to continue going back in the pool, even if you haven't found a swimming partner in a while. You have to steel yourself for the disappointments. For every 10 guys I go out with, there's only a mutual connection with one. You have to realize dating is a numbers game. Some people are lucky and find "the one" after meeting only a handful of people.

So know that you most likely will have to meet a lot of guys who on paper (in their profile and email) and on the phone seem like a good match. But when you meet, something critical is missing. (See my observations on this in "Signs that he won't be asking for a second date" and "First-date red flags that this guy isn't for you.")

Don't get discouraged. Keep diving into the dating pool!

What's the definition of a date?

I went to the movies with a guy I'd had a lunch date with a year ago. I told a friend, "I don't know if it was a date or not."

> *"Did he ask you to the movie?"*
>
> *"I don't recall. We talked a few weeks ago and the movie came up and one of us said it would be fun to go together and talk about it afterwards."*
>
> *"Did he pay?"*
>
> *"Yes, when I arrived at the theater he was already there and had bought the tickets."*
>
> *"Did you go somewhere afterwards?"*
>
> *"No, we just stood in the parking lot for a half-hour and talked."*
>
> *"Was there physical contact?"*
>
> *"Just a hug hello and goodbye."*

> *"Are you interested in him and he in you?"*
>
> *"I'm not sure. I like his mind, but I'm not drawn to him physically. I'm not sure what he thinks of me."*

Was it a date? Who knows?

Commonly, dates are meetings in which you are exploring if you might be a good romantic match. So is meeting for coffee a date? Most likely. Is lunch a date? Probably. Is dinner a date? Nearly always.

One man told me that his definition of dating was when you had met a person a few times and both decided you wanted to pursue a relationship. Others feel that just meeting and getting to know each other is dating.

The bottom line is, who cares what it's called? Just get out there and do it!

Fantasizing while Jazzercising

I Jazzercise two to three times a week. A while ago the class began in the church right next door to me. As a lackadaisical exerciser, I figured this was The Universe's way of saying, "You now have no viable excuse not to exercise." Even with a morning yoga class a block away, I nearly always turn over when the alarm buzzes to rouse me for class.

But Jazzercise is different. It's at the sane time of 6:00 p.m. And it's literally 50 feet from my house. It couldn't be closer unless the instructor came into my exercise room — which really should be called my "exercise equipment storage room."

The instructor is a big part of why I attend. He inspires me to keep coming back. Notice I say "he" — there aren't many male Jazzercise instructors, at least not in my city. He's 58 and not only cute, with a goatee and shoulder-length dreadlocks, but his buff, 6'4" lithe frame is chiseled from his 2-times-a-day classes. His wonderful bass voice sings harmony to the music. His easy smile lights up the room and makes the workout less odious.

Needless to say, sometimes it's difficult to focus on the dance moves. As he shakes his tush in his skintight jazz shorts and shirt, I get distracted. Sometimes I screw up the steps. His mocha skin reminds me of some of the yummy guys I've dated — past and present — and I can't help myself. I start fantasizing about their smooth skin, taut booties, rippling muscles, kisses, and … I'm grapevining left when everyone else is cha-chaing right.

I continue to attend, even though I have this tendency to trip over my own libido. As long as I don't start drooling, the gals in the class understand.

So don't underestimate where you can get your mojo going. Allow yourself to notice sexy guys wherever you are.

Dance through dating — and life

"Life may not be the party we hoped for but while we are here we should DANCE."

—Jerome Flowers

This quote is from my Jazzercise instructor's most recent newsletter. I thought it not only apropos as a life philosophy, but as a dating philosophy. I'm sure he meant this to be both literal and metaphorical as Jerome is part spiritual leader, part philosopher, part exercise psychologist, part Solid Gold soloist, part would-be professional singer and part playful imp. I described his joie de vivre in "Fantasizing while Jazzercising" on page 53.

Jerome is encouraging us to literally dance — even when we don't have a partner — because of the joy it brings us. Our body loves the movement, even if we don't consider ourselves good dancers. Dance anyway. In class, I sometimes feel awkward and klutzy watching Jerome's effortless smooth, sensual, natural movements. Ah, to dance like that — what a dream! But we each move our bodies in our own way, and it feels good with someone who is a patient, forgiving, natural to guide us, either as a dance partner or instructor.

I've taken to blasting the stereo and dancing to Barry White and others who help me get my groove on. Usually this is when I'm alone, often in my socks dancing around the kitchen while cooking dinner. Don't worry — I'm not imitating Tom Cruise in *Risky Business* in that I'm wearing more than a shirt, socks and undies. But the dancing can be as exhilarating as Tom's character expresses.

Jerome's line also reminds me of Lee Ann Womack's wonderful song "I Hope You Dance." In the refrain, she says:

> *"And when you get the choice to sit it out or dance, I hope you dance."*

Of course she and Jerome are reminding us to "dance" in life — to get out and do what you like and what feels good even if you don't have a partner, and even if you aren't particularly good at it. You'll get a smile on your face because you're enjoying yourself.

And who knows who might find you attractive because of it? But it really doesn't matter if anyone does, as you'll feel better about your life because you're doing something that makes you feel good.

In dating, if we haven't had a partner in a while, it feels like we can't "dance" — both literally and figuratively. We long to have someone to dance with to music and in life. But the truth is we can dance and still enjoy ourselves even without a partner right now. And advice I've read about attending singles dances says to dance by yourself — or at least sway to the music — near the dance floor and pretty quickly guys will notice that you are enjoying yourself and you'll soon have someone inviting you onto the dance floor. This works in life, too — when you are having a great time you attract others to you who want to share your fun. And of course, there's nothing to stop you from inviting someone to dance with you.

Make sure to download your free eBook Attract Your Next Great Mate: Dating Advice From Top Relationship Experts *at www.DatingGoddess.com/freebie*

Dating takes time

I continue to be surprised when people don't seem to understand that dating takes time. It takes hours to sort through potential matches, contact them, email and talk on the phone. Then there's an hour to meet them, if just for coffee. Dinner is 2-3 hours. A hike or bike ride, movie, theater, concert, dancing, etc., is many hours. Yet some of the guys I've talked to seem to have already over-full schedules with work, kids, friends, hobbies, working out, etc. So when do they think they'll have time to develop a relationship?

I dated a guy for 6 weeks who rarely made time to see me during the week, even though he worked less than a mile from me. When I'd suggest he come over after work for a drink or dinner, he rarely accepted, saying he was too tired and just wanted to crash. Early on, he made it clear that Fridays were his night with the boys, and Saturday daytime was for chores and errands. Sundays he spent with his daughter and Sunday nights he prepped for his work week. This left Saturday night. Period.

So how did he expect to develop a relationship in a few hours a week? He multitasked our phone calls during his commuting, so when he arrived at his destination the conversation ended. There was little consideration, I learned, for what I wanted. What if I wanted to see him during the week, go to a concert, movie, or just hang out? Too bad. We played by his rules or not at all.

Be honest with yourself — how much time each week are you willing to devote to finding and developing a love interest? Do you think you can just float into a relationship at your whim? That might be fine for those who just want a casual relationship or a booty call, but for someone looking for something long-term, it rarely works.

And if he isn't willing to invest some time, notice that early and move on.

What you perceive is what you receive

I've adapted a folk tale to dating.

> *On the outskirts of town, a woman was gardening next to the road when a stranger pulls up and leans out her window.*
>
> *"Hello there. I'm headed to your town to see if it would be a good place to resettle. I'm single and am looking for a place to find some guys to take me out. Tell me, what kind of single men live in this town?"*
>
> *"What kind of single men were there in the place you came from?"*
>
> *"What kind? Cheatin', lyin', two-timing, self-absorbed, immature, sex-obsessed jerks. I couldn't find one who was worth having a second date with, they were such losers."*
>
> *"Well," responded the gardener, "I reckon those are the kind of single men you'll find here."*

The stranger drove on, shaking her head as she called to the gardener, "Men are cads all over. All the good ones are taken or gay!"

The gardener went back to tending her flowers. A few hours later another woman pulls up. The driver gets out of the car.

"Good afternoon, ma'am. What a beautiful garden you have. I'm wondering if I might interrupt you a moment to ask you a question."

"Sure," says the gardener.

"I'm considering moving to your town. I'm single and am wondering what kind of single men are around these parts. What can you tell me about them?"

Those are the kind of single men you'll find here.

"Well," the gardener began, "what kind of single men were there in the place you came from?"

"Oh, there were many wonderful men. I went out with some lovely, intelligent, thoughtful, fun guys, many of whom have become treasured friends. I hated to leave, as there were so many

interesting guys to do things with. I wish I could have stayed, but I was transferred to this area and the opportunity was too good to turn down. I was having a great time, though, meeting some good, charming guys."

As she clipped a particularly beautiful rose the gardener said, "I reckon those are the kind of single men you'll find here."

"Thank you, ma'am. I know I'm going to like living here. I appreciate your input."

As she turned to leave, the gardener presented her with the rose.

Adapted from *The Woman Who Walked to Paradise* by Robert Stevens Fish.

Have you built a fortress around your heart?

If we've been hurt in love, it is easy to say, "I'm not going to let that happen again." We close off our heart, building a wall around it so no one can get close. The pain is too great. We don't want to feel like that ever again. We do whatever we can so that feeling won't be repeated.

When I was 40, I took a 9-day intense personal growth seminar. After a week of deep work we did an exercise that sounds particularly cruel. It certainly felt that way at the time yet it caused a breakthrough for me, but I would never recommend it.

The exercise was done within our group of 15 people who had been working together and sharing ourselves deeply all week. We were to choose the three people we felt least connected to and tell them so. This was excruciating for me to tell someone else this, but it was more so because half the group told me I was one of the three. I was so devastated I cried uncontrollably for a long time. In fact, it was so painful I get tears thinking about it now years later.

The breakthrough for me though, was to look at why I was causing such a disconnect with so many people. I always thought I got along well with most people, so this feedback was like a bucket of ice water on my head.

We close off our heart, building a wall around it so no one can get close

After much soul searching, I saw there were many reasons I was off-putting to others. But one that hit hard was that I'd built a thick wall around my heart, thinking that if no one got close they couldn't hurt me. Of course, all it really did was keep others — even people I loved — at arm's length.

I visualized myself kicking through the wall to expose my heart once again. After more work, I began to connect with those around me.

In *A Return to Love*, Marianne Willliamson says:

> *"Our barriers to love are rarely consciously chosen. They are our efforts to protect the places where the heart is bruised. Somewhere, sometime, we felt as though an open heart caused us*

> *pain or humiliation. We loved with the openness of a child, and someone didn't care, or laughed, or even punished us for the effort. In a quick moment, perhaps a fraction of a second, we made a decision to protect ourselves from ever feeling that pain again. We would never again allow ourselves to be so vulnerable. We built emotional defenses. We tried to build a fortress across our heart, to protect us from any cold assault. The only problem is, according to the Course [in Miracles], that we create what we defend against.*

Have you built a fortress around your heart so it is hard for love to get in? By breaking down the wall it means your heart is vulnerable, but without being open you can never fully love. Having your heart bruised is the risk you have to take to experience love. Are you willing?

Suffering is optional

When our dating activities don't go as we'd like, it is easy to get into a funk. We can drive ourselves crazy wondering what is wrong with us that we can't seem to attract anyone at all, or the men we do attract are disinterested in a relationship, have other afflictions, or we aren't drawn to them.

It is easy to be a suffering single.

Within days of my ex leaving I talked to a dear, wise friend for solace. I was wailing and complaining about what a louse he was to treat me this way. I wanted retribution for the pain he'd caused me by his decision. I wanted him to suffer as much as I was.

My friend said, "I can understand you would want him to feel the same pain you do, but he doesn't and won't. And for you, remember suffering is optional."

"How can suffering be optional?" I wanted to scream. "I can't control this feeling of a knife thrust into my gut."

No, I can't control that feeling. But I can control how I interpret situations — and whether I choose to wallow or for how long.

I remember I told myself I was going to just feel the feeling, just be with it and not make it right or wrong. I was not going to try to change it unless I wanted to. I also gave myself to the end of the year to mourn the loss of my marriage, which would give me a full 7.5 months to suffer however I chose.

As the end of the year approached, I noticed my suffering was nearly gone. I was looking forward to the new year to move on. I wasn't subjugating the sadness — I allowed it to surface when it did. But I didn't feel I was suffering in the sorrow.

We all have dating setbacks. We can choose if we suffer through them or not. It's okay if you do, but be clear that it is your choice. Sadness can bring gifts of release and insight. Suffering is really unnecessary. But if you want to do it, go right ahead!

When midlife dating is like high school

Perhaps you haven't dated in a while and now you're beginning to go out. You meet a guy who seems great and he seems to like you too. You have a good time together.

Suddenly you find yourself smitten. If he's said he'll call you tomorrow afternoon, you wait around the house all afternoon and evening hoping the phone will ring. If he calls, you're giddy with delight. If he doesn't, you worry about what you said or did that turned him off.

Maybe you discuss the budding relationship with your gal pals, asking their advice. If he hasn't called you when you think he should, you painfully debate whether to call him or not. Or perhaps you purposefully cruise places he frequents (gym, bar). Or maybe you find some lame excuse to drop by his place.

It feels similarly to how you felt in high school when you had a crush on a guy. Maybe you weren't even dating him, but some of your feelings and behaviors are the same. In high school, you detoured by his locker between classes, lingered outside the gym after his sports practice, and ate lunch near his usual hangout. You buddied up to his friends to find out more about him and his routines. Maybe you asked him to the Sadie Hawkins dance.

Is this healthy? The butterflies and euphoria of starting a relationship feel wonderful. However, if he isn't as interested in you as you are in him, those feelings will quickly morph into angst.

It becomes unhealthy when you find yourself thinking immature thoughts or behaving in ways that will embarrass later. A while ago I quickly became besotted with a man with whom I had dated only 3 times. I was obsessed with wanting him to call and called him more than I was comfortable. I heard myself thinking of asking him, "How do you want me to behave? What do you want me to change?" I was willing (I thought) to lose myself to be attractive to him. This is unhealthy!

Anytime you do something that you later are not proud of, you know you've gone over the deep end. The trick is to realize you're hypnotized by the fantasy of him before you act. If you find yourself wanting to do things that you know you'll regret later (e.g., sleeping with him as a way of keeping him), find a confidant to confess your plan and ask her to talk you out of it. If she lives nearby, maybe she'll come over and confiscate your car keys to make sure you won't do the stupid thing.

In her 40's, a friend chased after men with limited or no interest. She left her husband of 20 years and moved 2000 miles to the small town in which she grew up to be near her high school boyfriend. Unfortunately for her, he was happily married and had no intention of leaving his wife. She pined for him for over a year, periodically meeting him for a drink and frequenting his haunts to see him, even if he was with his wife. Eventually, he rebuffed her enough times that she realized her folly and let go of her infatuation.

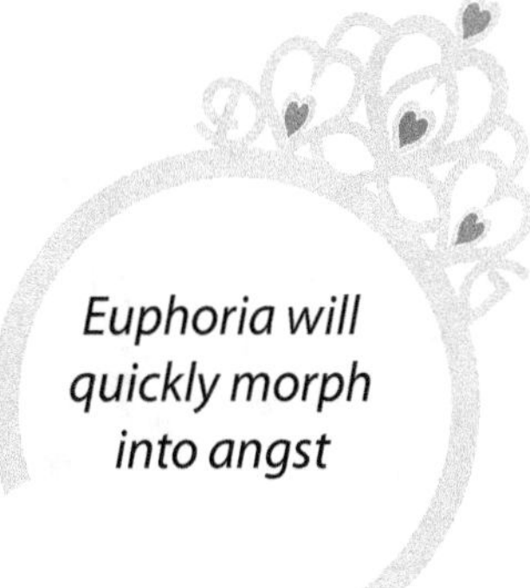

Another time she met a man who worked on a train. Within weeks of meeting him she moved into his train car that was attached to whatever train he was assigned to. She merrily fixed it up, sewing curtains for the windows and adding her woman's touch to make it more homey. They traveled wherever the train took them, crisscrossing the country. Within a few weeks, when they were many miles from her home town, he broke up with her and she had to find her way back home.

Perceived love can cause us to do really dumb things (in retrospect). Just like in high school. Our neediness, loneliness, or libido cause us to take immature actions. The key is to stop yourself before you do something you'll regret. Remember, you're not in high school anymore.

The sweet rewards of flirting

Usually flirting's rewards are putting a smile on someone else's face as well as your own, sharing a laugh and connection, enjoying the moment, and sometimes getting a hug, a kiss, or a date. But I've just received a new reward for my flirting.

A few weeks ago I was interviewed by a fun radio reporter. We've been keeping it up since then, emailing several times a week.

Imagine my delight and surprise to return home Sunday night from a business trip to have a box of Godiva awaiting from my "e-boyfriend," as he calls himself. My kind of man!

You may be thinking I've led this man on, since we've never met and barely talked on the phone. No, we've shared information about the people we're both currently dating. He said I've been "a fun muse." He added, "I've appreciated your sexy way of approaching life." He reads my blog, so knows my story.

So sometimes just the joy of flirting is reward enough. Or seeing the smile on the other person's face. And sometimes you get chocolate!

Flirt your heart out

"Flirt — a girl whose favorite man is the next one." —*Anonymous*

A friend asked me how to flirt. I hadn't really thought about it until she asked. So I looked at what I do that some find flirty. I am friendly, I smile at both men and women, and I say positive things to men. And sometimes I more overtly flirt.

Recently I was traveling and commented on the skycap's Southern accent.

"Where's your accent from?"

"Texas, ma'am."

"You don't sound like you're from Texas. You don't have that twang."

"Thank you, ma'am. I hate my accent and have been trying to lose it for years."

"Oh, no. It's charming. No need to lose it." I smiled.

Big smile: "You just made my day."

"I'm glad. By the way, is Tommy still here? He had braids and his son was also a skycap."

"I've worked here for many years and don't know a Tommy. However, my son used to work here and I had braids until recently. My son is now in college."

"You don't look old enough to have a son in college." I smiled again.

Big smile: "Wow! You've made my week now! Thank you very much. I hope you have a great trip."

With that, I walked away and we both had smiles on our faces.

Did it cost me anything to say what I said? No. Was I lying? No, nothing I said was a lie. Did I want anything from him? No. Did he feel better after our encounter? Absolutely!

So if you don't already, practice flirting. Now don't flirt with coupled men who you think will misinterpret it. I flirt with my gal pals' husbands in front of them. But I include them in the flirt: "Annie, you really scored snagging such a cute husband." "Laura, your hubby is so buff — how do you keep your hands off him?" "Sharon, you must be so proud to have such a successful husband."

Practice on waiters. Two gal pals and I were being

seated by the waiter who said, "And here is a special table for three beautiful women." I responded, "And we get to be waited on by a handsome waiter." Was he handsome? Not really. But he started it! I just wanted to continue the theme. I doubt that many women told him he was handsome. Did it cost me anything? No. And we got the best service ever — plus he comped us dessert!

So flirt with abandon with strangers. Practice with flight attendants, waiters, hotel staff, anyone who you feel won't think you mean more. It's fun. It will make their day, and yours, and when it comes time to flirt with someone who interests you, you'll feel comfortable, not nervous.

A lesson in non-attachment

The Zen story[1] goes:

> *In a mountainside village, a teenaged girl got pregnant. She was so terrified to tell her parents the truth that she told them the father was an old monk living nearby. When the child was born, the outraged parents took the baby to him and said,*
>
> *"This baby is yours," and gave it to him.*
>
> *The monk said, "Is that so?" and took the baby.*
>
> *Over the next few years he loved and cared for the child as if it were his own. The child flourished under his tender care, and he delighted having the child in his life.*
>
> *Meanwhile, the child's mother was overcome with remorse until she could not stand it. She finally admitted to her parents that her boyfriend was the child's father, not the monk.*

> *Her parents stormed back to the monk's cottage. Pounding angrily on the door, when he answered they demanded, "Give us back the child. It is not yours."*
>
> *The monk responded calmly, "Is that so?" and handed over the toddler.*

We could criticize the monk for not speaking up the first time. We could point out how he had no backbone and let people do whatever they wanted to him. We could berate the girl for bringing untold work onto the old monk. We could admonish her for shirking her parenting responsibilities out of cowardice. We could chastise the parents for their anger and judgment of the monk, without hearing his side of the story, then snatching away this child he'd lovingly cared for.

We could, but we won't, as none of that is the point of the story.

As I see it, the point of the story is to strive to live, as much as possible, in non-attachment. I know, I know, this is one of those much easier to say than do kind of things. The story is over the top in non-attachment. So let's bring it back to — of course — dating.

When you begin to like, be sweet on, or "kinda be likin'" (as my teenaged nieces would put it) a guy, it's natural to start to become attached. It's part of the emotional bonding that takes place in the formation of a committed relationship.

However, this attachment can go awry when you are first exploring each other. You may have emailed, talked on the phone and perhaps gone out on a few dates. You like him and he seems to like you. You begin to let yourself fall for him.

Then, poof, something happens and he's gone. Or his formerly nice, kind, attentive behavior has become aloof. He doesn't call as often, nor is he as complimentary. Instead of suggesting dinner out, now all he wants to do is bring pizza to your place with a DVD, knowing it will be easier to seduce you, and less expensive.

You get angry. It's easy to do. You feel he's led you on.

What if, instead, you said, "Is that so?" to whatever has happened. You just release him with as much compassion and kindness as you can muster. You remind yourself that you can get angry, but that doesn't change the situation; it only raises your blood pressure, which of course, doesn't affect him at all!

So try it. Whoever or whatever you are angry about right now, try just saying, "Is that so?" and move on. How does it feel?

[1]*Adapted from* The Woman Who Walked to Paradise *by Robert Stevens Fish.*

Dating can be addicting

There is the excitement of the chase. The first emails, phone calls, meetings. The attention of a man attempting to please you — to woo you. I'm often drawn to a man who says he wants to spoil his woman. I like being spoiled, don't you?

With online dating, there is a steady stream of potential suitors. Men write and tell you they are drawn to you: "You are smart, sexy, beautiful." Sounds good to me! I can't help it, I fall for these old lines.

Guys go out of their way to try to impress you. Just like you, they (usually) want to make a great first impression, so they are charming (if they know how to be), chivalrous, engaging. Not all men, of course, but more are at the beginning of the dating cycle.

When in between beaus, I've feverishly searched various online dating sites looking for potential matches. I've violated my own "don't initiate" rule (in the *Winning at the Online Dating Game: Stack the Deck in Your*

Favor book) and emailed interesting guys. To be without my fix of dating (e.g., attention) can be unnerving. You do what you need to do to score a flirty email or coffee date.

So beware. The dating dance can be habit forming. Watch out if you find yourself constantly searching the dealers (online dating sites), and be careful of doing things you know are not in your best interest (dating a guy you know isn't a good match) just to get your high.

Think of dating like the movie *Groundhog Day*

Remember the hilarious 1993 film *Groundhog Day*? Poor Bill Murray's character, Phil Connors, repeats the same day — Feb. 2, Groundhog Day — over and over and over again. But he's aware that he's reliving it so he begins to do different things each day, at first hedonistically. Then he begins to reexamine his life and priorities. He's sweet on Andie MacDowell's character, Rita, so he begins to learn what she likes, then woos her by pretending to like the same things until she falls for him.

It struck me the other day — not on Feb. 2 — that dating is an opportunity to do your own *Groundhog Day*. Instead of reliving the same situation with the same date, you have an opportunity to try something new with each guy.

For example, you decided you weren't straightforward enough with the last guy with whom you went out. You realized you should have been more clear with him about what you were looking for (e.g., a long-term relationship vs. casual dating). You two never went beyond him always calling you at the last minute for a movie and dinner. That guy is gone, so now you get a chance to do it differently next time.

With each successive guy, or even experience with the same guy, you have a chance to reflect on what worked and what didn't work, then to behave differently the next time. If it's with the same guy, you can see how your new behavior is received and whether the outcome is what you want or not. Just like Bill Murray's character, you can see how these new actions work and make adjustments for the next time.

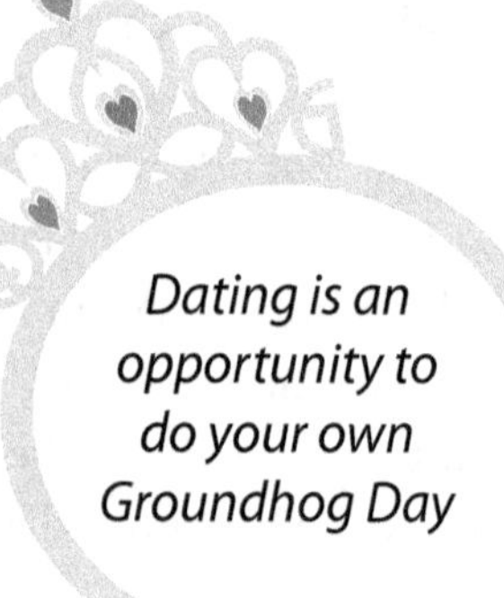

If it's a new guy, you can watch how your new approach works. Since every guy is different, the new behavior may work fine with one but not another. For example, if your fresh approach is to disclose on the first encounter your aforementioned purpose in dating, one guy may think it's great you are so clear and share that he, too, is looking for a long-term love, not a casual activity partner. Another may be impressed by your clarity, but share he has different needs. And another may be so threatened by your assertiveness that you never hear from him again. Good! You've now learned that your new behavior works to get rid of those who are threatened by you and attract those who say they want similar things. This works so well, you decide to bring it up in the pre-meeting phone conversation so those who don't want something similar are weeded out.

So look at dating life as a way to have your own personal continuous improvement program. Just as businesses are constantly looking at how to improve their processes and therefore their results, you have a grand opportunity to do this for your personal life. Look at it as a live training ground for you and use every opportunity to examine your own behaviors and outcomes and make adjustments the next time you're with a date.

What makes midlife dating different?

I'm often asked what makes dating in midlife different than dating in your 20's and 30's — at least for women. While I know the following are gross generalizations and there are always exceptions, here's what I've come up with:

- Having more/any biological kids is past. Most people are finished with the early part of child rearing, although some may want to adopt. Some people still have kids at home, some people's kids are grown, and some have grandkids. The biological clock has stopped ticking for most midlife women, which releases a tremendous amount of pressure from the dating process.
- Physical attractiveness has begun to wane. While there are still plenty of pretty/handsome midlifers, most have had some loss of beauty — at least from their perspective based on what they had in their youth. Many people are physically active, some even buff, and some in better shape than they were a decade or two

ago. But most have some wrinkles, and perhaps a bag or sag or two, unless there's been surgical enhancements. And some are more attractive with those signs of experience on their face.

- Health challenges may be present. High cholesterol, aching joints, high blood pressure and diabetes are common among midlifers, no matter how healthily you eat and how many days a week you work out. Much of this is managed through diligent diet, exercise and medication so it has little effect on activities, but some more severe cases limit activities. This makes dating more of a challenge when you have to explain why you can't go backpacking or windsurfing or rock climbing on your dates.

Midlifers are way more interesting

- Financial fitness is more common. Although divorce and health issues can take a financial toll, by midlife many people have figured out how to manage their money and often have financial security through investments. Even if they are not affluent, most have a strategy for getting by. And many can afford time off and grand vacations.

- More responsibilities make it harder to find time. Dating takes time. Midlifers are more likely to be looking after their parents and kids simultaneously. Add to that a job, physical fitness, friends and hobbies, and many don't have much time left over to devote to dating. However, if the kids are on their own and the parents don't need much attention, there can be plenty of time to explore activities with a sweetie.

- Clarity about what they want. After a break up or two, most people reflect on what they don't want to repeat. They are clearer about what they want their next relationship to entail. In fact, if someone has been married a time or two, in midlife they may decide they don't want to be married. Instead they may want an activity partner, but not someone with whom they will live.

- Wisdom about life. They may be slower to anger, quicker to forgive, mellower, more willing to love and be loved. Some people think midlifers are way more interesting to be with than younger dates, even though there is lots of hype about wanting boy/girl toys.

What can you add to this list that you notice about midlife daters and dating?

Are you sending "ready" vibes?

Talking to me about her dating life, a single friend said, "I'm really not ready, but I do have a profile posted."

"Why do you have a profile posted if you're not interested in actually dating right now?"

"It puts me in the mood of getting ready."

"That's wise. It opens you up to the possibility of dating, which carries over into real life. You send off more energy that you're available for romance and men pick that up. I've noticed more men flirt with me since I've been dating. I think it's my attitude."

Have you been getting ready to get ready to date? If so, why not take the plunge and post your profile on a site or two. If you get any nibbles and aren't quite ready, you can always politely decline. But it will also help you shift into ready mode more quickly. And who knows who'll pick up on those vibes and ask you out?

Ignore dating rule #1 at your peril

Rule #1 applies to life, not just dating. It earned its exalted status as #1 during a family reunion.

It was day two of the three-day reunion. Already those with "strong" (e.g., obnoxious) personalities were starting to get to some of us. A handful of us met for breakfast to have some nonirritating conversation.

It began with venting about what the "challenging" ones had said or done that got on our nerves. "How could he say that?" one asked. "If he would just learn to keep his mouth shut," responded another. After hearing the frustration others' behavior caused all of us, I had an epiphany.

"For our own sanity, we have to remember one thing: The only person you can change is yourself."

They didn't quite drop to their knees in reverence of this wise sage before them, but they did stop to consider the concept. We dubbed it "Rule #1" and agreed when another was frustrated with one of the vexing ones, we'd gently whisper "Remember Rule #1" in the ear of the stressed one.

It worked to not allow some thoughtless and unkind comments to escalate, as the recipient just breathed and focused on what she could do to shift her irritation.

What does this have to do with dating?

Many fights start after someone has gotten on your last nerve. Their irksome behaviors fester until you can stand it no longer. If this is a guy you're dating, it can be ugly and turn lethal for the relationship. Voicing your irritation — while you are irritated — can devolve into words that sever trust. Dating involves your becoming increasingly vulnerable, and if trust is broken, it is very difficult to repair.

The ideal is to reframe the behavior. (See "Turn your liabilities into assets" in the *Assessing Your Assets: Why You're A Great Catch* book and "Being 'in wonder' about your date's behavior" in the *Iron Out Dating Wrinkles: Work Through Challenges Without Getting Steamed* book) For example, a friend complained that her boyfriend sometimes tells her what to do. She could continue to get irritated at this behavior. Even after talking to him about it, he changed only slightly. So she has a choice: she can continue to get irritated and snap at him, or stop seeing him. Or she can think what positive reasons he might have for behaving that way.

For example, he wants his girlfriend to be successful at whatever she does. However, she's not a detail person so he's noticed she sometimes forgets the little things and then has to go back and fix them. He is more detail-oriented and sees the missing pieces. When he points out the missing details, he is trying to be helpful. He means well. In a twisted way, this is one way he shows his love for her. He's not implying she is stupid.

Now if he really thinks she's stupid, that's another matter. But if we are able to see the love under a behavior, it makes it easier to not get irritated.

Dating involves your becoming increasingly vulnerable

Granted, not all irritating behaviors are based on love. Some are a result of low social skills, low self-esteem, or psychological problems. The person is so wrapped up in his/her own world, s/he has no clue that what they said is hurtful or bothersome. And while I believe that as adults no one can verbally hurt you without your permission, there are times that concept is put to the test. When someone you care about and trust says mean things to you, it is hard not to get hurt.

Next time your date does something annoying, it is okay to talk to him about it — only when you're not still annoyed. (See "When do you tell your date about irritants?" in the *First-Rate First Dates* book.)

But practice seeing if it might actually be a way he's showing his connection or caring for you. If he continues to tell you lame jokes, realize his wanting to entertain you is his way of showing his affection. His expression of caring will take many forms, some of which aren't to your liking. If he's mature and sane, he'll want to focus on the actions that get the result he wants — your returned affection. But know that some behaviors that are irritating to you may have been encouraged by past dates/girlfriends/wives.

Make it a game you play with yourself to see if you can find something positive in the negative.

Midlife dating is like garage sale shopping

Do you like to shop at garage sales, swap meets, flea markets or eBay? I do. I've noticed some similarities to midlife dating.

Some friends eschew bargain shopping, as they say it reflects scarcity thinking. This could be true if you felt hand-me-downs were the only option for you — that you couldn't afford or didn't deserve brand-new merchandise.

I have a different perspective. I look at bargain hunting as a way to find treasures that others no longer have need for. I delight at rising early on Saturday mornings to capture the best goods. I see a parallel to midlife dating.

While some midlife daters are "brand new" — never married — most have been "used." Some have been "gently used" meaning their last relationship(s) ended with a positive feeling, if they have not been mistreated. Many times this is true when someone's spouse has died.

When you find gently used men, they are in good repair mentally — their perspective is positive and their outlook on women is healthy. These are the treasures we hunt for at the singles' swap meets (singles functions, online dating sites). Just as when I uncover highly valued items at garage sales, I delight to find men who no one else has discovered are available or a prize.

Sometimes I find a gem at a garage sale that is slightly scratched or in need of minor repair. These are overlooked by others because they don't want to take the time and care to polish the item to its former luster. Many midlife men are like this. They've had their heart broken or were treated badly by a woman — or women — so have some caution in their hopes for romance. But with gentle care, you can repair those minor cracks or gently sand away those scars. He just needs a little TLC to shine again.

And then there are the faded treasures that need a lot of refurbishing. Maybe they have been languishing, getting no attention, so have become rusted, faded, or fallen into disrepair. These precious items take your noticing their potential luminance and intrinsic value, as well as knowing it will take some effort and patience to make the piece/man sparkle once again. Some shoppers pass on these, knowing they don't want to put in that kind of time and work with no guarantee that the end product will be as magnificent as they hope. Others love the challenge and jump at the opportunity to apply their skills to help make this prize glisten.

Of course, in every garage sale there are those items that no one can find a need or desire for. You need not take pity on these, taking them home, intending to give them some attention someday. They will just continue to catch dust in your garage, attic, basement or closet. Best to leave them be if you have no intention of spending time on them.

He just needs a little TLC to shine again

But perhaps the garage sale/swap meet/eBay metaphor isn't the best to describe midlife daters. Perhaps we should instead consider that we're being offered at Christie's auction house, where only the finest previously owned merchandise is offered to discerning buyers. Just as with a dating site, there is a catalog with pictures, description and history. And we go to the highest "bidder" — the one who knows what it will take to capture our heart. But instead of an auctioneer deciding our fate, we have the power to say "sold."

Truth is stranger than fiction

I have had a few strange encounters during my dating adventure. None of them I could have imagined.

- I was contacted by a priest. His picture showed him in black priest attire and white collar! I assumed he is Episcopalian, but who knows?
- One guy brought a chaperone. In all fairness, the date was set on the only evening both of us had free that week. He called that day to say a friend had unexpectedly come in from out of town and would only be in town for the evening. Would I mind if his pal came along? I said, "That is fine, but what if I like him better than you?" He chuckled. It was an odd evening, and no, I didn't go out with either of them again.
- I had a date with a sexy, deep-voiced, cute guy who wrote alluring emails. His profile said he was "slightly kinky" and when we talked he

said he'd explain in person. I've learned that one person's kinky is another's normal, so I decided not worry too much about it until he explained. After sharing his background, including being an ex-Marine, he explained he was a cross dresser on occasion. Believe it or not, he was so charming that I didn't leave immediately. Instead, at his request, I shared how to put on pantyhose without running them, where to buy large-size strappy sandals, and the agony of eyebrow waxing!

He explained he was a cross dresser on occasion

So don't be surprised by who may show up in your life. Know what you're limits are in open mindedness.

Rejecting preconceived notions

Do you have biases about supposed characteristics attributed to a potential suitor's personality, values and behaviors based on limited information? For example, do you think lawyers are hard-nosed and bloodthirsty? Accountants are boring? Men over X age are sluggish and out of shape? Short men are…; tall men are…; men born abroad are…; men raised in certain religious traditions are….

No matter how open you like to think yourself to be, it is rare not to have some stereotypes based upon your experiences or your friends' experiences. Even if you feel you are unaffected by the media's depiction of certain professions, races, body types, religious backgrounds, etc., it is hard not to begin to lump men with similarities into some pigeonholes.

As open as I like to think I am to experiencing the person sans the stereotype, I'm not proud to admit I have had to confront my own preconceived notions.

And I've been delighted rather than disappointed when a man didn't match my negative stereotype.

A man I became besotted with taught me this lesson. When I learned of his former profession I had images of men who were accustomed to being in control, overbearing, gruff, and autocratic. I felt they were generally not in touch with their emotions and focused on getting their way. Having had few personal interactions with those in his profession, my images were from television shows and movies featuring his ilk.

So imagine my unbridled delight to learn he is humble, thoughtful, kind, generous, gentlemanly, highly intelligent, tender, articulate and caring. Nearly the opposite of all the clichés I'd held.

The lesson is to not assume someone is like others you've encountered — even if you've not actually met someone of his kind, just seen them in the media. If you allow an open mind, you may be very pleasantly surprised to learn the man has qualities you adore rather than the odious ones you assumed.

Are you enjoying the banquet of dating?

World class photojournalist, author, and former National Geographic photographer Dewitt Jones is also an entrancing speaker. His presentations are illustrated with his riveting photos as he makes his points on creativity, leadership, vision and passion.

In a presentation I heard over 15 years ago, one of his phrases still reverberates: "The banquet is laid, though nobody comes.*" When I recently asked him about it, he said, "I use it to refer to the banquet nature/God sets before us every day." Yet, as he points out, we are often too stuck in whatever is in front of us to step back, look around, and see the bounty of beauty before us.

A banquet often involves a buffet — a display of yummy food from which we choose. We are given the opportunity to not only select known favorites, but to sample items we might not normally pick. If we try the new fare, we may come back for seconds and add it to our list of delectable delights.

When women tell me they haven't gathered the gumption to start dating even though they want to, I think of Dewitt's line: "The banquet is laid, though nobody comes." The "banquet" is a plethora of interesting men to be met, and among them, we hope a delectable delight or two. Ideally one who will become our all-time favorite and last a lifetime. Yet many are afraid to start, settling instead on their current lives — as fulfilling as they may be — even though they long for a mate to share their lives and add a dimension they feel is missing.

Of course, I'm not suggesting that to be single is depriving you of the banquet of life. We are using the metaphor here specific to dating. Dewitt uses the phrase in the context of enjoying the beauty of nature. I'm using it to encourage those who are a trifle trepidatious about tapping the terrific treats of dating.

Think of the banquet that awaits you

If you've decided to get back into the dating scene but haven't yet made the next move, think of the banquet that awaits you. Just as at a banquet, not every "dish" will be to your liking. Dating allows you to "taste" dishes you might not have tried before. Don't turn down an invitation from someone who doesn't meet 100% of your criteria. If he's 85-90% what you're looking for, at least have coffee. Even if you aren't drawn to him — or vice versa — you can now say, "I've tried X and it isn't to my taste." But if you don't even allow yourself to try something new, how will you know?

But know that perhaps one of these "tastes" will result in your establishing a new preference — something you may not have thought you'd like. I thought I'd only want someone with a certain type of job. But I've become fond of someone who works in an industry that wouldn't have been on my desired list.

So get out your plate and be willing to go through the banquet line with an attitude of openness and inquisitiveness. You never know what delicious bounty you will discover.

** This loosely references Luke 14:23 from the Bible.*

Approaching dating like a buffet

A friend asked if there were any new interesting men on the horizon as I reenter the dating scene after a meltdown with a beau. I shared that an intriguing sounding man showed up in my online matches. He's a graduate school professor at a nearby internationally renowned university. I said, "Even if we're not attracted to each other after meeting, I think he'd make a fascinating coffee date."

She said, "I wouldn't think of meeting with someone just because he sounds interesting. I look for signs of shared values, background, interests, sense of humor or other indications we might be a match."

When looking at an online dating profile, it's hard to tell much of anything about the man. But if there are several elements that you find interesting, why not at least respond to the match?

In some ways I approach dating like a buffet. When I partake in a smorgasbord, I'm interested in tasting some new dishes, trying things I probably wouldn't order from a menu. The same with men. I use online dating as a way to meet men who sound interesting. And just like at a buffet, I take a small taste — a coffee meeting — to see if I want more. If I like what I've sampled, I can usually go back for more (a second date).

Knowing you aren't making a commitment for a whole meal before you know if you'll like it makes it easier to try new dishes (men). You can allow yourself to experiment. If you never thought you'd like a bald man but never dated one, try a man who seems a match on many items but happens to be hairless. Thought you had a limit for a man's height? Try an extra-tall guy if all else seems good.

Now, just like a buffet, you can get heartburn if you taste too many options in a short time. Balancing men, just like balancing an overloaded plate, is tricky. So only take on what you know you can juggle. Once you find something you like it is sometimes hard not to want to continue tasting. But at some point you decide you've had your fill of new dishes and choose one favorite.

I've expanded my choices by being willing to try something different. Know that there are abundant possibilities available and you can perhaps uncover a new taste treat you wouldn't have found if you weren't willing to experiment.

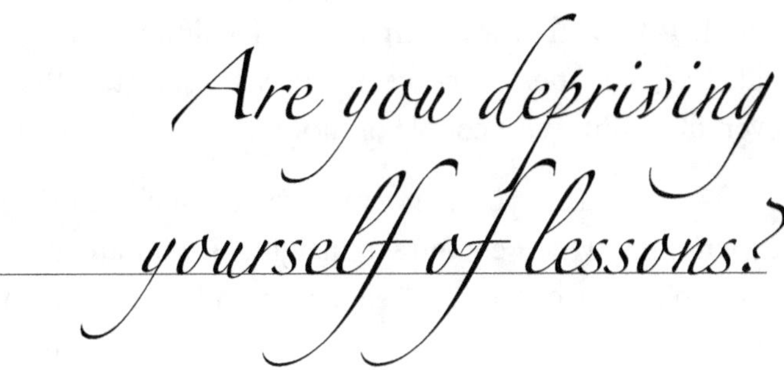

Are you depriving yourself of lessons?

The other day bestselling author Sam Horn* let loose with a sage saying:

> *"You can't learn anything from experiences you aren't having." —Louis L'Amour*

I immediately thought of the women who've said they would like to date but can't quite get up the gumption to do so. People look at dating as a chance to meet potential love interests. However, there also can be a lot of learning about yourself during the process, at least if you're willing to be reflective and present to the lessons each encounter offers.

So while you may think not dating isn't costing you anything, it could very well be costing you some key lessons about yourself and being in a relationship — even a possibly fleeting one like dating. I know I have learned a great deal from my 3.5 years of dating, not only about myself, but about men in general. I have a greater appreciation for how amazing it is that two people get together in the first place, let alone the work, patience, and perseverance it takes to stay together, even for as little as a couple of months.

By not dating you are depriving yourself of having experiences which encourage insights. If you are at all conscious, introspective, reflective, and honest with yourself, by dating you have prepared yourself to be a much better mate after having dated for a while and with a few men.

By not dating you are depriving yourself of experiences which encourage insights

A popular question in the "getting to know you" stage is, "What did you learn after the breakup of your last relationship, and how will you apply it to your next one?" If your last relationship was decades ago, will those lessons be fresh? Will you be as conscious of your patterns that can cause problems? Will you have had an opportunity to practice new behaviors that mitigate the past problem areas?

I realize that not everyone is "ready" to date. If you know you have some healing to do, then it is wise not to reenter the dating pool until you feel mostly healed. But if you wait until you absolutely, positively have no more relationship wounds, you may be dead before you're ready. Most people carry some residual pain from past relationships, and being in a relationship can actually help speed the healing, even if it also triggers some old heartache. Many times these emotional ghosts help us look at the hold old sorrow has on us, and if we know how to do it, we can release it.

What are some of the lessons you've learned about yourself and relationships from dating that you can apply to the next one? And what experiences are you holding back from that you know you could learn from?

* Go to www.SamHorn.com for more on Sam Horn.

Is Brad Pitt ruining your love life?

Recently I saw *Ocean's Thirteen*. It was an eye-candy feast, with George Clooney and Brad Pitt 25 feet high. Yum!

We know how effective media is in shaping our perspective, even our values, including our self-image. We know that being bombarded with images of beautiful men and women molds our vision of attractiveness. As we mature, we know it is fantasy and that even Hollywood beauties don't look that stunning without professional hair, makeup, wardrobe and lighting.

You've probably seen the Dove video called *Evolution*. It shows how an attractive woman morphs into a fabulous knockout through professional hair, makeup, lighting, and yes, even Photoshop.

How do these unrealistic images affect your dating?

1. They can influence your expectation of a man's looks. Very few men, let alone midlife men, look anything close to the 46-year-old Clooney or the 43-year-old Pitt. So while we realize

these men personify an unattainable ideal, some small part of many women want — and perhaps expect — their guy to look as yummy.

2. The Photoshopped images of pencil-thin specimens on magazine covers and in movies exacerbate women's feelings of inadequacy. In Ocean's Thirteen, Ellen Barkin portrays a model-thin woman prancing in low-cut, tight dresses with 3.5 inch heels. How many real-life 53-year-old women do you see looking like that? Just as women have unrealistic expectations of a man's looks, so, too, men have an idealized expectation that women look like these air-brushed fantasy females.

So it is a lose-lose for both genders.

We think (hope?) that as one matures, people realize that these movie-star looks are really just fantasy. But unfortunately, I've found both men and women who hold themselves and their potential dates to standards that nearly no one meets in real life.

How do you feel the media's images of near-perfect people effects your expectations, both of your own looks and those of your potential partner?

Who are you magnetizing into your life?

Some folks believe they attract people into their life. Within reason, I'm one of them. I don't believe that I attract every person with whom I come in contact, but I do think I've had important people come to me, if even for just a few minutes. When that's happened, there's been a lesson for me from my interaction with them.

I feel the same way about the men I draw into my dating life. I've enjoyed meeting nearly all the men with whom I've had at least coffee. Some have turned into beaus or treasured pals. And even the few who weren't pleasant had a lesson for me.

This concept of attraction is articulated in Richard Bach's *Messiah's Handbook*. I love most everything Bach has written. He has a knack for being pithy and profound simultaneously. The quote I'm referencing is:

> **Master's Certificate**
>
> *This is to certify that the bearer has been declared a Master of Spacetime, and is authorized*

to command absolute control over all personal life events and an indefinite number of simultaneous life experiences, to focus consciousness among them at will to freely choose triumph or tragedy as she or he wishes, and to magnetize such like spirits as she or he desires for her or his personal education and entertainment. This certificate is subject to the following limits: Self-imposed.

It's there, that certificate, in everybody's pocket.

I love this concept that we magnetize people into our lives who we desire for our "personal education and entertainment." That does not mean we use people for our own pleasure, but since the other person has the same certificate, we are there for his/her amusement or education as well. It's mutual.

When you realize you are drawing people into your life — especially men who you meet to explore possible romance — your perspective shifts. You look at the man sitting opposite you with new eyes. What is he there to teach you? Don't worry about what you are there to teach him — that's his job to figure out.

In ""There must be a pony in here"" (page 133) I quote another of Bach's aphorisms to remember when the encounter isn't as positive as you'd like.

What do you think about the dating partners you've drawn to you? Do you see the lessons they've brought? Or were they there merely for your amusement?

The midlife dating hero(ine)'s journey

Recently I watched the DVD "Joseph Campbell: The Hero's Journey" because I wanted to know more about his work. In *The Hero with a Thousand Faces*, Campbell codified thousands of years of myths from multiple cultures into what he described as The Hero's Journey. Star Wars, Matrix and countless other movies and stories follow this outline.

Since my writing is predominantly for women, with apologies to Campbell, I'm going to call it *The Heroine's Journey* and we're going to examine how it applies to midlife dating.

While the stages of the journey are not always the same, they generally follow this path:

1. A call to adventure, which the heroine has to accept or decline. In dating, this would be reentering single life, whether it was by your choice or not. (Sometimes in myths the hero/heroine did not choose the adventure.) Just

as in myths, the heroine may not consider her new situation an "adventure" at first.

2. A road of trials, in which the heroine succeeds or fails. We would call these first dates. ☺ Or perhaps they are relationships gone sour. In order to advance on the path, you must face these trials and develop skills and knowledge as a result.

3. Achieving the goal or "boon," which often results in important self-knowledge. While you might naturally think the goal of dating is to find your next mate, it could be better knowledge of yourself and what you want in a mate. The dictionary describes "boon" as "a thing that is helpful or beneficial." Insight and better self-knowledge are always helpful.

The heroine may not consider her new situation an adventure at first

4. A return to the ordinary world, again as to which the heroine can succeed or fail. The "ordinary world" for us would be, perhaps, entering into an exclusive relationship. And just as in myths, this can succeed or fail. Or the ordinary world could be your being fine with

being single and dating — or not dating — as you please.

5. Application of the boon, in which what the heroine has gained can be used to improve the world. You use your newfound insights, lessons, and skills to better communicate, have more empathy and patience, and make this relationship work. Or you more readily see it's not working, discuss it and decide whether to stay or move on.

Where do you see yourself in The Dating Heroine's Journey? I see myself moving through steps 2-5 repeatedly and becoming wiser with each excursion.

It is all about you

A friend shared that in a moment of candor one of his mentees disclosed he was first put off by my friend, in part because that day my friend's shoes didn't match his pants. My friend explained to him that sometimes he doesn't pay as much attention to those details as he should, but he didn't get defensive. He said it launched an insightful discussion into the types of things about which his mentee was judgmental. He said, "I was clear my mentee's comment wasn't really about me, but about him."

Yes, it was. Anytime we are triggered by something another does, it is about us. The mentee's comment created an opening to explore why he was judgmental about something as minor as a clothing mismatch.

Whenever I'm reminded of an insight generator, I like to see how it applies to me. After all, it is all about me! (Just as these things are about you, too, if you care to look.) I asked myself what dates I'd rejected because of minor things, perhaps not shoe/pants mismatches, but things like table manners, lack of chivalry, unconscious comments. Was I, like the mentee, making more of these hiccups than I should? Did I reject some good guys because of seemingly small things?

My justification is that even minor indiscretions are indicative of core behavior and beliefs. If a man doesn't call when he says he will and has no viable excuse, I declare him inconsiderate. If he doesn't help with my coat, he's unconscious of manners. If he wears wrinkled clothing on dates, he doesn't have pride in his appearance. The list goes on.

On the other end of the spectrum of responses to these behaviors is just to notice and accept them without judgment. I don't live on that end of the continuum very much. Of course, it is easier to accept a man's idiosyncrasies if you know you're not interested in a long term relationship with him — or if you aren't married to him!

Did I reject some good guys because of seemingly small things?

The challenge comes when our rationale for rejecting him is clearly so "right." Of course you feel justified not accepting a second date since he didn't bother to iron his shirt to make a good impression on you. But some women wouldn't even notice. And ironing is a fixable issue and you may be rejecting a charming, loving, affectionate, loyal man over an issue that a laundry service could easily solve. This is about you because of a notion that the man you want to be with would have the good sense to wear ironed clothes, even though you overlook other stellar qualities to focus on a sub-par superficial one.

In your dating adventures, what behaviors from your dates have triggered something that allowed you to look deeper into your motivations, values and behaviors?

Sometimes it's about you; sometimes it's not

In dating, it's easy to take things personally if there are problems or hiccups. Sometimes the guy you're seeing does or says something that is a reflection of his attitude toward you, and you take offense.

But often his behavior has nothing to do with you. It's harder to realize this when he attributes positive feelings to you that would be impossible to come by after only a meeting or two.

I learned this when a man I went out with once told me he loved me at the end of the date. It happened again yesterday.

This man and I went out twice four months ago. There wasn't the spark I needed to see each other romantically, so we decided to be just friends. We kept in touch periodically via phone and text, but I haven't heard from him in a month.

Yesterday he called and was flirtatious. When I said it didn't sound like how friends talked to each other, he asked what I meant. I reminded him of our conversation and said I was seeing someone else. He said he has no memory of that conversation and was crushed. He said he envisioned us being together for a long time, that I was so much of what he'd been looking for, that he loved me. He started to cry, saying he can't believe how he screwed this up. I told him I had no idea he felt that way and tried to console him.

On one hand, I could be flattered that he felt this way about me after so little contact. On the other, I'm realistic enough to know that no one could fall in love with another after only a few encounters, especially if there was not clearly mutual attraction.

No one could fall in love with another after only a few encounters

I realized that this scenario really had little if anything to do with me. It was really about a lonely man feeling he'd made a connection and idealizing me without really knowing me. It can happen to any of us, as we see through the lens of what we want to see.

The lesson is to ask yourself, "Is this really about me? Or is it about some need he has that he attributes to me?" It will keep you saner in dating if you understand not all that we see is based on the other, but more through the filter of our own needs.

"There must be a pony in here"

It is often hard to stay so upbeat in the face of many dating encounters that haven't panned out. It can sound exciting to have gone out with a lot of men, but it is also time consuming and frustrating.

One phrase that keeps me going is from Richard Bach's book Illusions: The Adventures of a Reluctant Messiah. You may remember Bach from Jonathan Livingston Seagull. Both were packed with thought-provoking philosophy wrapped around an engaging story.

In Illusions, Bach says, "There is no such thing as a problem without a gift for you in its hands. You seek these problems because you need their gifts." When you look at the problem as bearing a gift, you search for it.

When you have a less-than-grand encounter with a date, learn to look for the gift. There is a needed lesson if you are willing to search. Ask yourself some questions:

1. *Why is what he did/ didn't do bothersome to me? What do I make it mean? Do I make it mean something about me?*

For example, if he kisses you passionately in public, do you interpret that as his not having respect for you? Thinking you're a trollop? Why do you care as long as you know you're not easy?

2. *What is another way to interpret his behavior?*

With the passionate kiss, he could have felt such overwhelming affection for you that his desire to kiss you won out over any sense of inappropriateness. You could feel flattered that he is so attracted to you that he couldn't wait to express it. Isn't that part of romance — feeling so full of passion you want to express your love everywhere?

3. *Did his behavior trigger a hurt from a previous time in my life?*

If so, you're not upset with the current man, but from a past encounter that hasn't been healed. Maybe someone from the past kissed you passionately in public. That experience coupled with other behaviors left you feeling disrespected. If the current man hasn't shown other signs of disrespect, you shouldn't burden him with the same hurt feelings that belong to the past guy. This trigger gives you an opportunity to explore the past hurt and heal it.

4. *What signals am I sending that say this behavior is okay?*

If you are playful, flirty, affectionate and accepting, are you encouraging him to show public displays of affection and he doesn't yet know what is beyond your comfort level? Did you tell him it isn't comfortable for you and he persists?

5. *What do I do that is irritating to him, yet don't know it yet?*

Do I make it mean something about me?

If you put on lipstick at the dinner table and it drives him batty, how would you know unless he mentioned it? And how do you want to be told so you can offer him feedback in a similar way, at least until you know how he wants to receive such feedback?

5 *Is he being a mirror for my similar behaviors?*

For example, say you don't like it when people interrupt you. But occasionally you find yourself interrupting others. So is he unwittingly reminding you why people might not be able to wait to express their thoughts?

Whenever someone does something you find annoying, ask yourself if you do the same thing or something similar. You may find sometimes you do, so their behavior reminds you to rein in your own.

So just like the joke about the child who enters a room full of manure and exclaims, "There must be a pony in here somewhere!" you can look for the hidden gifts in any encounter. The key is to believe there is a gift and to be willing to look for it, even if it means something not so great about you.

Timing is everything

You know the old adage that the secret to comedy is timing? The same is true in dating.

We seek the mate of our dreams. So we date. And we date. And we date.

We get frustrated. "Why can't I find a great guy?" we ask ourselves. We get tired of going out on dates that go nowhere. Maybe we get bitter.

You have to ask yourself if you believe a great guy for you is out there. "Yes," you respond.

You ask if he's looking for you. "Yes. Unless he's currently married. Then he'd have to get divorced, then find me."

Can you speed up the process? No. You don't know when or where you'll meet. But you're certain you will meet. You don't know if it's today, next week, or next year.

You have a choice. You can get frustrated and perhaps resentful about something you can't control. Or you could enjoy the process and relax. Meet interesting men, as you never know if the next one is your guy. Notice the positive characteristics in the guys who aren't a match for you. Ignore and forgive the ones who don't have the social graces to exit thoughtfully or treat you right.

He's looking for you as hard as you are looking for him

And have faith that when the time is right you will meet your guy. He's very likely looking for you as hard as you are looking for him.

Rules for Responsible Dating

Wouldn't it be great if there were rules for responsible dating, just as there are rules for responsible driving? I realize not everyone abides by responsible driving guidelines, but at least some have been publicized so more people do than if nothing had been created.

So how about we craft some rules for responsible dating? Let me begin, and you can add what I leave out:

Rules for Responsible Dating

- You will only date if you are not in a long-term relationship. No dating if you are married or living together, unless you have the explicit permission of your partner.
- You will only date those with whom you want to explore a long-term relationship, unless you

both are explicit about seeking only a casual or intimate encounter.

- You will be honest about your age, marital status, height, income, body shape, health and other facts about you and your life. If someone misinterprets some key information (you are separated and s/he thinks you are divorced), you will correct the misunderstanding immediately.

- If you decide you no longer want to see someone, you tell him/her gently, honestly and as soon as you make the decision.

You will be honest

- You will not make promises you don't intend to keep ("I'll call you" or "Yes, I'd like to see you again"). You don't avoid the person nor not return their calls if you don't want to see him/her again. You address it maturely and responsibly.

- When someone says they don't want to see you again, or they would like to just be friends, you graciously accept that they aren't a match and let go.

- You will never, ever, ever, stand up anyone. If you are unexpectedly detained or decide against the meeting you will call the person's cell phone and/or the meeting site to inform him/her as soon as you realize you won't make it. The same goes for being more than 5 minutes late — call. The only viable excuse is if your home/office is aflame, you have been kidnapped, or you or a family member has to be taken to the hospital.
- Before becoming intimate, you initiate a conversation about safe sex, STD tests and protection.

Midlife dating etiquette

The other day I was asked me for some rules of etiquette for when one is beginning to date. While etiquette is, according to the dictionary, "the customary code of polite behavior," there are no hard and fast rules. What is rude to one is not a big deal for another. Following are what I've heard are common complaints from both genders. You may not have a challenge with any item, but I think it's important to know what may be considered good- or ill-mannered by another.

Both genders:

- Respond promptly to online contacts, even if you're not interested. Don't let someone linger in limbo. If you're not interested, send them a kind, "Thank you, but we're not a match" email. (Some people think no response is better than an outright rejection, but the majority of people I've talked to about this would rather hear a polite "no thanks" than nothing at all.)

- When on the phone, give the other your full attention. Don't grocery shop, watch TV, read your email, or surf a dating site. I experienced the latter during an initial phone call with a potential suitor. At first I was impressed that he was referring to items on my profile; then he digressed to reading me emails he'd received from woman wanting to make contact.

- When together, don't answer your phone, unless you've specified in advance that your child or boss may call. If you do answer, make it very brief, not "No, I'm not doing anything. What's going on with you?" Believe it or not, I've heard this from people over the age of 40 on a date. If the call is going to be more than a 30-second "Let me call you back in a few hours," excuse yourself and take it outside.

- When face to face, give the other your focus. Don't check out others as they walk by. We can see your eyes look people up and down! The same is true at a party or bar where you are looking over the person's shoulder.

- Be on time. In fact, being a little early is even better. You can then stake out the quietest spot, as well as observe the posture, walk and attire of the other. I met a man once who had arrived early and staked out a table, so I didn't see him walk in. Only when I picked up something I dropped did I noticed his both pants legs' hem had come unsown so were ragged and dragging on the floor.

- Get cleaned up. That means wearing neat, clean, ironed, well-fitting clothing in good repair. Brush your hair and teeth before the meeting. Take a shower that day.
- Don't be critical of the other. It takes a long time to develop enough trust to be allowed to give critical feedback.
- Don't talk about other people you are dating. When you disclose you are seeing others, you don't need to give details, even if asked.
- Don't lead on the other if you have no interest.
- Limit your discussion of your ex(es) and try to find a way to say something positive about him/her. If you're only bashing, you'll sound bitter and negative, which is unappealing.
- Share the conversation, don't hog it. Think of questions about the other that you want to know. Work to not ask the same questions every other person has asked your date.
- Don't talk about sexual topics before meeting or on the first date.
- Limit your alcohol consumption to one or two drinks on the first encounter. Alcohol impairs your judgment and you may make decisions you'll later regret.

- When you've decided you don't want to see the other again, have the courage to say so as pleasantly as possible. Don't take the coward's way out and stop responding to emails and calls.

Women:

- Don't practice arbitrary rules, like only having one contact with a man per day. If you both like to email or call a few times a day, do it. Don't limit yourself by what some "expert" says to do — including this one.
- Don't accept a date with a man you have no interest in just for a free lunch, dinner, or concert.
- Do not put on lipstick or make up at the table. Excuse yourself to the ladies' room.

Men:

- Pick a first rendezvous spot where you'll be comfortable treating. While it is the 21st Century, the norm is still for the man to treat on the first date unless the woman has made it clear she'd prefer to go dutch. Coffee dates are perfectly fine for a first meeting. Don't feel you have to go to a fancy place to impress her on the first encounter.
- Brush up on gentleman's etiquette: ask her to order first, open doors, walk by her side, not in front unless it's in a crowd. Know which fork to use, which glass(es) and bread plate are

yours, and when to put your napkin in your lap (when you first sit down). Buy a book on male etiquette from your local independent bookstore.

- Don't ask out a woman you have no interest in just for a sex, unless you're positive that's all she wants, too. Ask, don't assume.

Everyone can benefit from an etiquette review every once in a while, just as they could from a driving review. Don't assume you have nothing to learn. Ask your opposite sex dating buddies for what bugs them about the your gender during dating.

Can ducks help you find love?

When in Singapore recently, I learned about a Chinese legend that is supposed to help you attract love. It's pretty simple.

In Chinatown, a friend pointed out two Mandarin duck figurines. She said if you put these little statues in your bedroom so they faced each other bill-to-bill, they would attract love to you.

Why?

In feng shui, Mandarin ducks are regarded as a symbol of conjugal affection, fidelity, happiness in love, romance, devotion, togetherness and enduring love. They are often used in Chinese weddings because they symbolize wedded bliss as, I was told, they mate for life.

My friend assured me that if I had these figurines in my bedroom, my true love would enter my life. It worked for her just weeks after she put her pair in her bedroom — her sweetheart of the last four years appeared.

I neglected to buy a pair on my last trip, but sought them out when I was back in Singapore recently. This time I wasn't after them for attracting love, since I'd found my beau. However, I thought these kissing ducks would be a fun way to encourage love persisting.

I bought two sets of duck statuettes — one for me and one for my guy. When returning home, I immediately set my kissing ducks on my headboard. When my beau came over the next day, I told him the legend and how they are supposed to help our love last. Then I gave him his pair. He immediately said — "I'm going to super glue their bills together." Cute, very cute.

"I'm going to super glue their bills together"

So the next time you're in a store with Chinese decorative items, ask if they have any Mandarin ducks. Buy some, put them in your bedroom — bill to bill, of course — and see what happens!

The purrrrfect partner

I had a new guy in my bed last night. He was sweet, affectionate and cute. He begged and begged. It's not the first time I've fallen for a persuasive male. However, I didn't even know his name until the morning when we awoke wrapped around each other. And I didn't learn it from him.

While staying at a friend's house, her cat Calvin insisted on sleeping with me. I welcomed him. His soft purring and luxurious fur were irresistible.

It made me think of what we do when men are beguiling. Perhaps it's their looks, their attention, their feel, their soft words of adoration — whether sincere or fake. Sometimes we can be easily persuaded. They reward us for our attention with affection we may be craving. They are responsive to our touch, they verbalize their approval. In fact, several men have literally purred when I stroked their hair or gave them a shoulder massage.

And just like cats, some men can be aloof when they've received what they want. Calvin jumped off the bed when he heard other voices, seeking his next affection provider. She may not have been nicer, prettier, thinner, needier, buffer or younger. She was just perhaps more available than the still-drowsy me. Some other woman who was happy to stroke him, talk sweetly and give him the care he wanted.

Cats and men disappear for their own reasons. Some come back when they want what you provided. Others are gone forever when they find a handler who makes life easy on them. It's not you, it's him. Enjoy what you've got when you've got it. And release him fully when he disappears. Clutching at him will only result in his claws coming out and your getting scratched — physically or emotionally.

Dating angels

What is a dating angel? No, not the person you are dating — although some of them can be angelic. A dating angel is a stranger who helps you feel good about yourself. Someone who gives you an emotional lift, who flirts with you, or who leaves you feeling attractive after interacting with them.

For example, I was sitting at a stop light one warm summer day leaving a lunch date. My windows were down, my stereo blaring Marvin Gaye. I was seat dancing to the beat. I was "dated up" — make up, hair, etc. A man pulled up to my right. His window was down, so he noticed I was singing with Marvin.

"Hi," he said. I turned and smiled,

"Hi."

"Have you had lunch?" he asked.

"Yes, I just came from lunch."

A dating angel is someone who gives you an emotional lift

> "Darn. If you hadn't, I'd ask you to have lunch with me."
>
> "Sorry," I responded, and smiled as the light turned green and we went our separate ways.

He was a dating angel. The lunch date had been okay, but the guy wasn't a match. Neither was the guy in the car, but he bolstered my ego.

Another dating angel was the older woman in Macy's who approached me while I was shopping since I was 15 minutes early to meet my date at the mall entrance. "I just have to tell you how great you look," she offered. Since strangers — especially women — don't approach me and say things like this, I asked her to repeat it, thinking I'd heard wrong. Nope. She repeated the same sentence. I smiled and thanked her. So it was with an extra spring in my step that I greeted my date.

Dating angels can be servers in restaurants, people you pass on the street who smile at you, or people who outright flirt with you just to flirt. One day when I was wearing a straw hat I smiled as I approached an older gentleman on the sidewalk. He commented, "You look marvelous in that hat." That made my day!

So be on the lookout for your dating angels. They're out there if you just open your eyes and ears. Appreciate their presence. And you can be a dating angel for someone else, too, even if they aren't dating.

When lost baggage is a good thing

We all carry some baggage — as in emotional baggage — when we date and enter new relationships. We all schlep some from past hurts with lovers, parents or others who were influential. Sometimes we haul hurts inflicted by strangers.

I'm a little wary when a potential suitor says he has no emotional baggage — unless he is the Dalai Lama, but I bet even he would say he has some (being the enlightened being that he is).

I've borrowed a phrase I read in some wise man's profile, "I've gotten my baggage down to carry on size." I love this as it says you know that we all have baggage and that while much of yours is released, you know you still have some lingering issues to work through.

The challenge is to be aware of the baggage you have left to release and make your partner aware of it, too. Then he can know if your reaction is to him specifically or to some past pain.

Some people think they don't have baggage, so don't know there's anything left to release. If you get upset about something trivial, like traffic, bad drivers, someone a few minutes late, then you have baggage. You need to work through why these minor irritations cause you strife. No doubt, it's linked to something in childhood where you felt you weren't understood, were dismissed, humiliated, or felt unloved.

Some people think they don't have baggage

Start noticing and perhaps logging what triggers you on your dates. If he's late, do you make that mean he's a flake and disrespects you? If so, that's baggage. The truth could be he got caught in traffic or just didn't plan well enough. Start noticing and losing your baggage — on purpose.

Falling in love is like cocaine

Psychiatrist Daniel Amen said, "Love is a drug. Falling in love is like taking cocaine. It works in the same center of the brain."

We all know that falling in love is euphoric. In "Dating can be addicting" (page 85), I likened it to drugs. I had no idea a scientist would come to the same conclusion!

In the height of "love season" (Valentine's Day) most of us think, at least some, about love. Whether it's toward a sweetheart, your friends, or family, love is definitely in the air.

Most of the conversation and images about love, however, usually center on the heart. Intellectually we know that the brain is the source of our feelings of love, but we don't say, "I gave him my brain," we say "I gave him my heart." Nor do we express, "I was brain broken," but instead say, "I was heartbroken."

From his book, *Sex on the Brain: 12 Lessons to Enhance Your Love Life*, Dr. Amen says,

> *"The vast majority of love and sex occurs in the brain. Your brain decides who is attractive to you, how to get a date, how well you do on the date, what to do with the feelings that develop, how long those feelings last, when to commit, and how well you do as a partner and a parent. Your brain helps you be enthusiastic in the bedroom or drains you of desire and passion. Your brain helps you process and learn from a breakup or makes you vulnerable to depression or obsession.*
>
> *"While plastic surgeons, diet gurus, and the pharmaceutical industry may have convinced you that they hold the secret to a fulfilling sex life, the truth is that you already have the only thing you really need: a brain. As the largest and most sensitive sexual organ in the body, a healthy human brain enhances your sex life and heightens sensation. A troubled brain, however, makes emotional and physical connection with others difficult. So forget the implants, the fad diets, and the pills. Learning about this intriguing and sexy organ is the key to your sexual satisfaction."*

Great news, huh? Instead of killing ourselves at the gym to look hot, I guess we just need to exercise our brains!

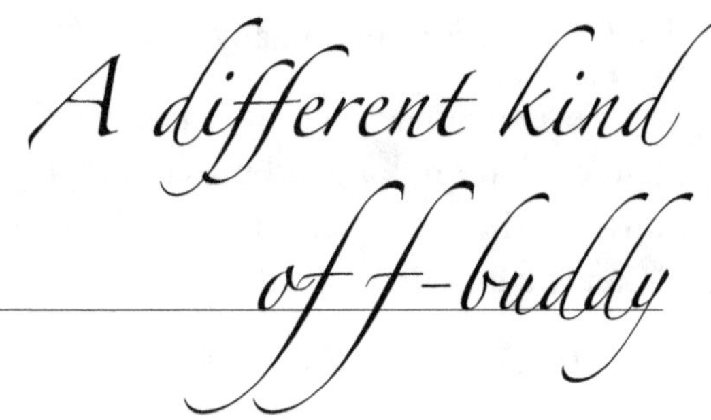

A different kind of f-buddy

No, I am not referring to the term most commonly associated with the f-buddy phrase. I have a new meaning for f-buddy — flirt buddy!

What is a flirt buddy? Someone with whom you can flirt by email, phone or in person who knows you have no serious intentions. Some of my favorite flirt buddies are married men whose wives know that their husbands and I flirt.

One f-buddy even called his wife over to listen to a flirty voice mail I'd left him where I asked if he thought she might allow me to be his "extra" wife since he was so financially smart that I was sure he could afford two. She howled with laughter, saying "That girl has no idea what she'd be in for."

Yesterday I had lunch with another, whose wife has not met me but knows a lot about me. He shared that he told her exactly where he'd be and that she could call during lunch if she wanted. She didn't. She knows he —

and she — are safe from any indiscretion with me.

Several single men have become f-buddies, as we know we are not a good match but enjoy playing and flirting. They are often the same guys I go to with my, "Can you explain why a guy would…?" questions.

I think flirting is key to dating, especially when getting to know someone by email and phone. If you can't flirt — without going over the line — it is hard to show your interest, at least until you meet face to face. If you can flirt, it gives the other a smile and giggle. As long as it's not smarmy.

Have trouble knowing how to flirt? See "Flirt your heart out" (page 77).

What do you think of flirt buddies?

The scent of love

A male friend is convinced that smell has a lot to do with dating attraction. He believes people exude a human pheromone of sorts, functioning as an attractant of the opposite sex. But since pheromone receptors have not yet been found in humans, what scent does attract us?

Some women believe perfume is an attractant, so they slather themselves with it. They don't realize that most men abhor being with a woman who reeks, no matter how expensive the perfume. (Men can go overboard with cologne as well.)

In the 1992 film *Scent of a Woman*, Al Pacino's blind character is drawn to the woman with whom he wants to tango by her smell. This was so powerful, it became the title of the movie.

I've always thought a whiff of a subtle fragrance was appealing. The idea is to emit an alluring aroma that entices my date to get nearer. Once at the end of a first date, my dining companion and I hugged goodbye. When we disengaged, I noticed his eyes were closed and he took a deep whiff. "I love how you smell, " he whispered.

I've wondered what scents would be irresistible wafting toward my date's nose. My ex loved vanilla, so I'd raid the kitchen cabinet and dab a bit behind my ears when I wanted to drive him crazy. Now I've come upon a different universally drool-inducing smell that gets most everyone's attention. But I can't find it in toilet water form. What is it?

Fresh-baked chocolate chip cookies.

When you pass a Mrs. Fields store, doesn't the smell — which is purposefully fanned into the corridors — beckon you, just as the Sirens to Odysseus? Don't you want to stop and buy, or at the minimum, just enjoy the smell? Most people do.

What scents would be irresistible wafting toward my date's nose?

So why doesn't someone package that smell? It would ensure you'd be followed by men — and probably some women — like a fishmonger trailed by cats. Then you wouldn't have to worry about going to singles bars, speed dating, or online dating sites. You'd have a parade of men following you and you could merely pick and choose from among the masses.

Of course, you may have trouble shaking the ones you reject. You don't want to encourage stalkers just because your scent is irresistible. Maybe you could carry a skunk scent aerosol can to spray behind the man/men you've chosen, to separate the selected one(s) from the riff raff.

So, I'll let you know when I've developed eau de chocolate chip cookie. I'm sure you'll want to buy it by the gallon.

(Epilogue: I was at a conference a few days after I wrote this and discussed this concept with a male flirt buddy. He said he'd definitely be driven crazy by eau de chocolate chip cookie. Serendipitously, a few minutes later the afternoon break refreshments arrived — chocolate chip cookies. I took one over to him and rubbed it clearly on my neck. He took the bait and started nibbling away — on my neck, not the cookie!)

Truffles, pigs and romance

You may have heard of the pheromone androsterone, found in boar saliva, that is similar to what men secrete through sweat glands. It is said to drive some females into a frenzy. Did you know that truffles (the wild mushroom kind, not the chocolate kind) smell similarly? Truffles' scent is what makes sows such effective detectives to root out the expensive vegetable (reportedly one of the highest-priced foods in the world).

So why don't men slather androsterone — or truffles — on themselves before going on a date? If the effect on women is similar to how sows in heat react to boars women would be throwing themselves at them. Women try for the same effect by wearing low-cut tops, mini-skirts and fishnets and it seems to work much of the time!

Well, good news for us, ladies. We can't be manipulated quite that easily, with either mushroom truffles, chocolate truffles, or androsterone. According to a National Geographic Smell Survey, 30% of humans cannot detect androsterone unless the concentration is extremely high. So he'd have to bathe in it to become the babe magnet of most men's fantasies. And even worse, a random sampling of 100 people found that around half will detect nothing, 15 or so will smell an inoffensive musky-floral-woody aroma, and the rest will be thoroughly repulsed by a liquid that, to them, reeks of stale urine or particularly nasty body odor.

Some men wouldn't mind the risk of being repulsive to 35% of women in order to attract just a few. I couldn't find data on the percentage of women who are attracted to this scent.

I found a few products that included androsterone. I'd be curious to hear reports from those who tried it. Did women flock to the man's side, start ripping off clothes, throwing phone numbers, attacking him in crowded buses? I think this would have made the news. So either not many men are trying this, or again, we're safe.

What do you like to smell on a man? And what scent would be a sure bet for you to wear? I've explained my nomination in "The scent of love" (page 161).

"Date #75 requests permission to land"

Passing the airport the other day, my friend Ken noticed the many planes lined up for miles in the sky awaiting their turn to approach the runway. He said he immediately thought of my always having an endless stream of potential suitors lined up in various stages of "landing" a date with me.

I'm never long without someone knocking on my fuselage

It's true that I am never long without someone knocking on my fuselage, I mean email door, wanting to make contact. The value of having guys lined up is I don't linger over love gone sour. Much the same as when I miss a flight, there is nearly always another one ready to take off within a short period.

Just as some of the planes in queue may have to circle in a holding pattern if the runway is busy, so too a potential paramour may have to wait his turn if I'm besotted with someone else at the moment. Of course, just like an air traffic controller, I can deftly juggle several flights at once.

And similar to when a pilot may have difficulty landing in severe weather or with wind shear, sometimes too, a first date can be shaky. It takes a confident, experienced pilot to safely maneuver in unfamiliar conditions, like a first date with someone she barely knows.

If the landing is too rocky and uncomfortable — unnerving even — then I quickly disembark and wish the pilot well as he takes off on his next journey without me. So, too, with rocky dates — I know this man is not for me, so I bid him good luck and say bon voyage.

And sometimes I choose to just hang out in the terminal, or no one is in a landing pattern. That's fine, as I busy myself reading, calling friends, writing my next book or blog entry, viewing a DVD or just people watching. A favorite game is picking out potential boyfriends from the airport crowd, deciding with whom I'd want to go out.

Then pretty soon I hear a new pilot saying, "Dating Goddess's Date #75 requests permission to land." And the next adventure begins.

Belief in a wreath

I recently read about a Lithuanian summer solstice ritual where at midnight unmarried women toss leaf and flower wreaths into rivers. The belief is that their wreath will be pulled out downriver by the man of their dreams.

If only it was this easy to telegraph to the man of our dreams that we are available and awaiting his appearance!

While I admire their intentions, the execution leaves something to be desired. My romantic nature clashes with my practical side. Too many issues arise for this matchmaking technique to be plausible.

- This process assumes my future mate can swim, or at least has a long enough pole and sufficient ability to snare my wreath from the river. I have no idea if Lithuanian rivers are fast or slow moving, but if the former, he'd better have some quick reflexes. Since this ritual occurs at midnight, he would have to not be an early sleeper, or else set his alarm to get to the bridge in time to snag my wreath. And unless there are torches or spotlights scanning the river, he'd better have great night vision, something most of the midlife men I've dated can't claim. (Perhaps my dream guy is much younger with good eyesight and a strong swim stroke. Hmm. That could be fun.)

- How would he trace my wreath back to me? Would I attach a laminated luggage tag with my cell number or business card? Or would he ride his white horse (better yet, white Mercedes) from upstream village to village holding my bedraggled wreath asking all unmarried-looking women if it was theirs? What would prevent my sisters in singlehood from saying "yes" even though it wasn't, just to hook him?
- What if he lived far downstream? Would he have the patience to wait until 1:00 or 2:00 a.m. before he hooked my wreath? If so, then this would be a good portent as he wouldn't yell when he picked me up for a date and I took a tad longer than expected.

There are several versions of this Lithuanian ritual. One has single women bathing in the dew (just how would one bathe in dew? Lay out a towel or wash cloth the night before so it was saturated?) or rivers, as they believe on this day bathing in these sources increases one's beauty. (If this were true, I'm sure Esteé Lauder would be bottling this and selling it as "eau de dew.") In some places girls wake before dawn to wash in the dew and return to bed hoping to dream of their future husbands. I'm afraid I'd never be able to participate in

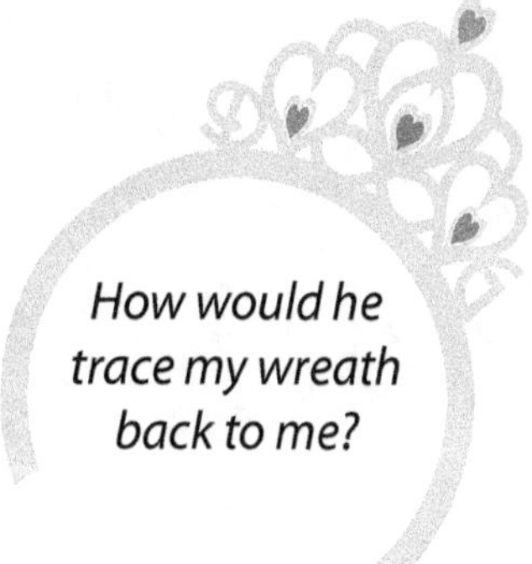

this version of the ritual as I rarely arise before dawn except to catch a plane, never to catch a man, or even a glimpse of my future one.

Another version has both men and women floating wreaths intertwined with candles in the rivers. If the wreaths of a woman and man float together, it is a sign that they will wed. So I'd need to be careful what guys are standing around me as they are most likely to have wreaths that commingle with mine.

While my cynical nature wants the data on how many Lithuanians have found their life partner this way, if I were in Lithuania on the solstice I would defiantly drop my wreath in the water. I'd hope my guy had good night vision, an accurate snaring arm, and Bond-like sleuthing ability to find me.

Being a good Girl Scout in dating

I loved being a Girl Scout. On meeting days I proudly wore my uniform to school and voraciously earned many badges to decorate my sash.

Recently, I thought about how The Girl Scout Law affects my dating — and of course, my life philosophy. In it, girls are encouraged to do their best, be honest, fair , helpful, considerate, friendly, caring, respectful, and responsible, and "make the world a better place."

One of The Girl Scout Law concepts came up with a beau. He'd sent me a picture of him with a goatee. I commented how good it looked on him, and how I thought goatees were sexy. The next time I saw him, he was starting a goatee! (It really did look good on him.)

He also wears glasses. I casually asked if he'd ever worn contacts, which he said he had. He asked why I asked, and I told him his eyes were pretty and they stood out more when he didn't wear his glasses. He said he'd update his contact prescription and start wearing them when we went out.

I am sensitive to couples trying to change each other. I am torn between just liking a man as he is or suggesting little tweaks that he doesn't see and would make him more attractive, effective, or successful. But I'm clear that one shouldn't try to remold a man to become someone he isn't.

However, The Girl Scout Law line of "I will do my best to make the world a better place" I think applies to the guy you are dating if you can suggest small modifications that will be better for him in the long run. When I was in Girl Scouts, I remember the concept as "leaving any situation better than you found it." That could be picking up trash on a trail, cleaning off a dirty table, or giving someone a sincere compliment.

So if you suggest something that you like but isn't a fit for his personality or job, that is not being "considerate and caring," another of the tenets, nor "respecting others" — him.

Perhaps we could modify The Girl Scout Laws to be "The Positive Dating Laws" as they seem to fit dating perfectly.

"I will do my best to make the world a better place"

Do you follow any of The Girl Scout Law concepts in dating?

Approaching dating as a project

A potential suitor and I talked about the process of dating. He said he's been put off by women who are assertive (aggressive?) about their dating time line. On the first date, he's been told by more than one woman that she wants to be married within the year and begin a family soon afterward. They have their life plan mapped out and are just missing one thing — a man.

I said they approaching dating as a project. So we played with the various milestones one would list if you were creating a project plan for your next love. Tongue in cheek, here's my fleshing out the concept.

Project milestones for finding mate

1. Find prospective mates.
2. Narrow down the list.
3. Make first contact (either initiate or respond). If online dating, via email.

4. Talk on the phone.
5. Set up first date.
6. Have first date.
7. Decide if there will be second encounter. If not, go back to #1.
8. Go on subsequent dates.
9. Have first kiss. (May be concurrent with #6.)
10. Progress with physical affection and emotional bonding.
11. Decide to become exclusive.
12. Sex. (Hopefully, this comes after #11.) If not satisfying go back to #1.
13. Go away for the weekend. (#12 may be concurrent with this.)
14. Meet his/her friends. (This may come before or after #12, 13 or 15.)
15. Meet his/her family. (This may come before or after #12, 13 or 14.)
16. Go on vacation together.
17. Move in together.
18. Become engaged. (This may come before #17.)
19. Marriage. (This may or may not follow #18.)

20. Kids (or not). (This may or may not follow #18 and 19.)
21. Death or divorce (If his is the former, or if the latter, go back to #1.)

What milestones have I left out?

Treasures can come in dented packages

If you received a gift in a Tiffany's box but the corner was mushed, would you be unhappy? If you were given a 2-pound box of your favorite Godiva with the top indented, would you be disappointed?

No, of course not. Because you know it's what's inside that really matters, not the packaging.

Many midlife daters make snap decisions upon meeting a potential new suitor based on a minor physical imperfection. Perhaps their date is carrying a few extra pounds. Or their glasses are out of date. Or they don't have the right colored hair.

The *Washington Post* plays matchmaker each week setting up two singles who, based on their application, seem to be a match. *The Post* interviews each dater afterward and reports each dater's thoughts. Recent reports after each Date Lab experience showed that nearly all those interviewed were not drawn to the person physically, although their personality was a match.

It's amazing to me how we make such judgments about if it will work out or not before the other person has opened his mouth. However, I know I'm guilty of this myself. A friend recently pointed to a man across the room with whom she'd been talking and discovered he's widowed and looking for a new relationship. He said things that she thought would be a good fit for me. But when I saw him I said, "He's not my type." So I was being as shallow as those quoted above!

On the other hand, nearly none of the men I've dated for more than a few times would fit my physical description of my ideal man. My ex was good looking and I was drawn to his looks even when he was in his 60s. I can say that about just a few of the men I've dated since. I commonly think, "If I were to see him across the room at a party, I wouldn't be pulled to meet him."

However, there was something there to make me want to see a man again and again. If I could get past the lack of immediate physical attraction, I'd often find a treasure inside. And the more I fell for the treasure, the more attractive he got.

So even if a new guy doesn't meet all your physical requirements, give him a chance to expose his inner gems. He may just become as yummy as those Godiva chocolates!

Do potential suitors leave an impression on you?

After National Public Radio host's Scott Simon ended his interview with actor/singer Terrence Howard, they walked out together. Scott said, "As we were leaving the studio … he grabbed my arm. 'I touch you, my fingers leave an imprint,' he explained. 'The shape of my fingers will disappear. But maybe something I said will live on. Something you said to me will live on.'"

So it is with the potential suitors with whom we share an email, phone conversation, coffee, or more. If we listen carefully and ask thought-provoking questions, their answers may give us insight into relationships, men, or what you want or don't want. Your questions or answers might do the same for them.

I've learned lessons from men I've never met, just talked to on the phone, sometimes just once. Some of these conversations have made indelible impressions on me for their insight, wisdom, or astuteness — or sometimes the lack thereof. If we approach every encounter with openness to whatever lesson may be revealed, we live a richer life.

Sometimes the conversations reinforce something we already know. Other times the man tells us volumes about his values and character which either compel us to want to know more, or repel us to know we aren't a good match. Even the latter, however, leaves an imprint — a lesson for what to ask in the future.

Be grateful for the imprints others have left on you as there is learning in them all. The wisdom you receive will live on. And know that you have left a lasting impact on men you've encountered.

(Listen to the full interview of Terrence Howard. Mr. Simon says, "I have interviewed thousands of actors over the years. None have been as eloquent, illustrative, or fascinating as Terrence Howard." http://tinyurl.com/6frxcp)

You have to buy your dating ticket

Some midlife women have shared that they would be interested in dating and finding a sweetie, but they don't want to do any work to find him. They may — or may not — list themselves on a dating site, but they're not willing to look at profiles, nor email anyone. If someone approaches them, they may or may not respond.

Some have actually said, "I'd love to have a guy in my life, but he would have to find me at the places I like to hang out."

This reminded me of an old joke I'm sure you've heard.

> *A woman prays to win the big lottery. She doesn't and wails at God. The next week the jackpot is bigger, and she prays more, but again doesn't win. She shakes her fist toward the sky expressing her disappointment and anger. Another week passes, the fund has grown still larger. She prays and prays and prays to win.*

> *She does not. In her frustration, she cries and exclaims, "God, why have you forsaken me! I need that money. Why can't you help me win?"*
>
> *A voice from on high booms, "You have to buy a lottery ticket."*

Are you "buying" the dating equivalent of a lottery ticket? Are you doing anything to find a guy? Are you online, telling your friends to set you up, going to singles' dances, or joining singles' activities clubs? Are you expecting your next love to trip over you at Curves? In the Nordstrom lingerie department? At the Macy's makeup counter? At a beading class? I don't think a lot of guys frequent these places.

Some women don't want to vary their routine at all to see if they can meet a guy. Why not take a class on something that interests you but is guy dominated? I once took a class on auto mechanics because I wanted to know more about how my car ran and minor maintenance I could do. There was only one other woman in the class. I didn't date anyone from the class, but at the time I was going with someone.

I don't have a recipe for how to find suitable guys. But I do know if you only go to work, Curves, quilting class and stay home watching TV or DVDs, I doubt he's going to find you. Unless he's the pizza delivery guy, your mail carrier or the UPS delivery man.

So don't complain if you don't win the guy lottery. You have to buy a ticket or not even God can help you.

Do you have time to wait to open your heart?

A friend died unexpectedly. When someone passes it prompts us to reflect on what's important. Loved ones always appear at the top of that list. We become more appreciative of the gifts around us: a friend's call, a sunny day, fresh-baked cookies, a child's laughter, a warm hug, a beautiful sunset, a full moon rising.

It also helps us put things in perspective. For example, this week I struggle with whether to surrender to a strong attraction and let myself fall into intimacy. One pal's advice: "Wait to go there. All good things take time."

But what if there is no time? Who knows when something will happen to any of us? Shouldn't life be embraced fully and savored? Are you an eat-dessert-first kind of gal or wait-and-enjoy-it-in-time? I am a bit of both, but I find myself becoming more of the former.

A pal said that I was "fearless." Often when people point out what they perceive as my courage, I don't see it as such. (See "Courage and dating," page 33) I'm merely acting from the question, "What are my options?" I have the option to date or not. While I can entertain myself or with pals, there's nothing like the embrace and kiss of someone who enchants you. I'm not willing to live without that for long. So I get "dated up" and have coffee dates with men who seem interesting and intelligent. Most end up just as coffee dates, but some become more.

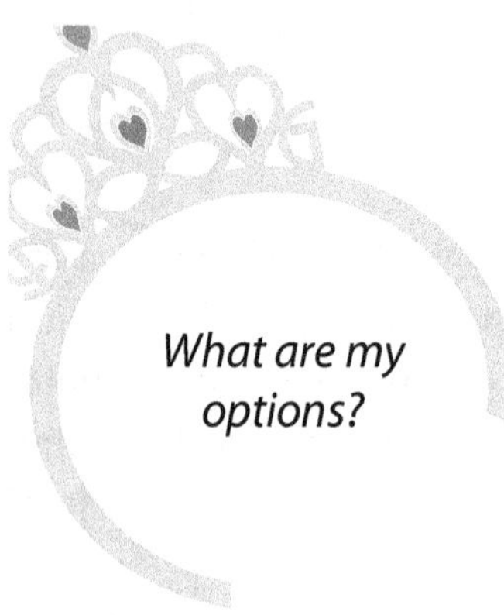

Jane Juska's book *A Round-Heeled Woman: My Late-Life Adventures in Sex and Romance* helped shift my perspective. (She put an ad in The NY Review of Books which read "Before I turn 67 — next March — I would like to have a lot of sex with a man I like.") In her book she describes how she wanted to experience the pleasure of a man's caress and seduction before she got too old to enjoy it. It made me see that I'd made arbitrary rules based on my fears and doubts, not on living life passionately.

Are there rules you've made about dating that need reassessing? Perhaps the rule was made after a painful experience and has limited your living fully because of fear of being hurt. Life and love are full of hurts. Hopefully, the pleasures far outweigh them. You can't prevent all hurts by rules. But rules can prevent you from embracing life. If you've closed your heart how can anyone get close enough to love you?

Imagine you only had a year or two to live. How would you live and love differently? Would you allow yourself to be open to loving fully?

A few years ago my aforementioned friend remarried in his late fifties to a wonderful woman who adored him. He enjoyed her devotion and love for him and she shined in his. Now he is gone. If he had not opened his heart and allowed himself to love and be loved, he would have died without experiencing this midlife passion.

Take off any shackles that hold you back. If you need some therapy to let go of your fears, call a professional now. You never know how long you have.

Dating with "Beginner's Mind"

The term "Beginner's Mind" comes from Zen Buddhism. It means having an open mind, an eagerness and a lack of preconceptions when learning about a topic or activity, even when you aren't a novice.

Midlife dating can be difficult to approach with a childlike wonder because you've dated in the past and/or been in long-term relationships. You feel you are at the graduate level, not a newbie. You think you know a lot about the other gender, even if you've had difficulty in many of your past relationships.

The key element of this approach is that in the Beginner's Mind there are many possibilities; in the expert's mind there are few.

Here's a story that illustrates this concept.

A learned man went to visit a famous Zen master under the auspices of wanting to learn more about Zen from the master. As the master quietly prepared tea, the man pontificated about Zen. On and on he went arrogantly sharing what was "right" and "wrong" with the philosophy. When the master poured the visitor's tea, he continued pouring past the brim. The man watched the overflowing cup, yelling at the master, "Stop! It's overfull! No more will go in!" The master looked at him calmly. "You are like this cup. How can I show you Zen unless you first empty your cup."

So it can be with dating. If we think we are so advanced that we know all there is to know about ourselves, men and relationships, there is no room for new information. We pontificate: "All men want is sex," "Men are jerks," "All the good men are taken." There is no room in our world view to see that men want more than just sex, there are lots of wonderful, available, non-jerk midlife men wanting to find a great woman like you.

There are lots of wonderful midlife men wanting a woman like you.

So how do we approach dating with Beginner's Mind? The first step is to be aware of what preconceptions are in our mind already and be willing to let go of the beliefs that keep us attracting men that aren't a match and repelling men that are. When we release old beliefs that no longer serve us, there is room for messages that will get us what we want: a loving, interesting, honest, loyal man.

When you hear yourself thinking a negative stereotypical thought, actively work to say, "I am open to believing a different interpretation." For example, you hear of a man cheating on his girlfriend, you think, "All men are players, cheaters and pigs." Consciously change that to, "A few men are cheaters, but I know that the majority of men are loyal, honest and caring. That is the kind of man who is attracted to be with me."

What makes it difficult for you to approach dating with a Beginner's Mind? What negative tapes keep playing in your head that you think limit you from approaching dating with enthusiasm and wonder?

Are you emotionally ready to begin dating again?

A 7-year-divorced, midlife friend is starting to date again after a few-year respite. A few years ago, she fell in love with a man who seemed equally infatuated. They dated for six months, having sleepovers several times a week. It seemed this relationship was going to be long-term, so she took the plunge and introduced him to her teenage daughter, something reserved for very few of the men she dated.

On a business trip, immediately upon landing she turned on her phone to tell her sweetie that she'd arrived safely and there was his text: "I'm married."

We can only imagine the pain, anger, betrayal, hurt, and confusion she felt. Needless to say, it's taken her a while to reenter the dating pool.

Which she did recently.

She shared, "I met someone online. I liked him but since I'm so rusty, I was nervous on the first date. He gently put his arm around me and I couldn't believe I said, 'Don't touch me! You don't know me well enough.'"

Now we feel compassion for her, don't we? We understand how one can be nervous around someone whom they've become fond through emails and phone conversations. A kind, loving, caring man would give her some grace because of the pre-meeting connection they'd shared.

But her story doesn't end here.

"A few seconds before my blurting out at him, I tensed up, clutching my arm to my body. My phone, which was inside my pocket, randomly dialed my daughter's friend. She heard me tell him not to touch me and thought I was in trouble on this date. She proceeded to call everyone who she thought knew me to tell them something was wrong on my date. So everyone started texting me and warning me to stay put and someone would rescue me. Poor guy, he thought I was completely nuts."

Oy! She's now testing every ounce of patience he has. Any deposits she had made to his Bank of Grace are close to being — if not already — overdrawn.

She didn't share how this date ended, or if it ended right then, or if she ever talked to him again. But I understood — and I think she did too — that she wasn't really emotionally ready to begin dating again. Her nerves were a bit too raw and her ability to graciously express her boundaries was nonexistent.

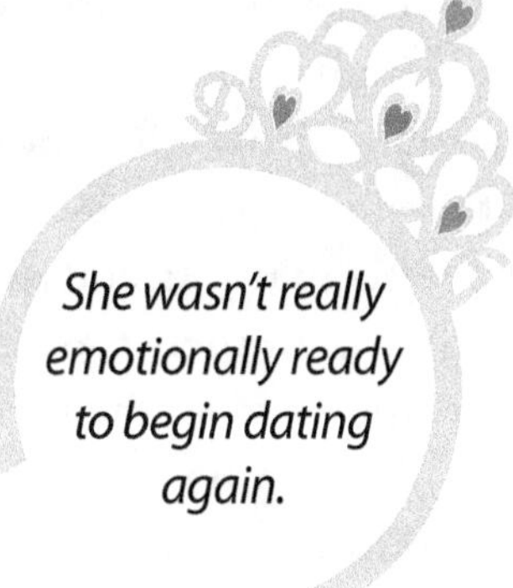

What could you do if you find yourself similarly unable to cope? Admit it. If a man does something that unwittingly crosses your boundary (e.g., first date hand on knee, passionate kiss, or other PDA), you can simply say, "I haven't dated in a while and it will take me a little while to get to know you and feel comfortable with PDAs." Or, "I'm a bit rusty at dating, so I'd like to take it slow." Or, "I love PDAs but I have to know a guy a bit longer to feel comfortable."

My friend is an intelligent, sensitive, thoughtful woman, so I'm guessing that after she pulled away she said something like the above to him. And hopefully he/they could laugh at all the texting drama. It could happen to any of us.

No matter on which side of this scenario you might find yourself, it's telling to see how each person reacts. If she didn't apologize for her brusqueness, that says a lot about her. If he didn't accept it, that tells us a lot about him. If she didn't laugh at the texting and say something like, "It's great to have so many friends who care about me," she's taking life much too seriously. (And she needed to respond to all the texts to assure her friends she was fine.) If he didn't laugh along with her, he's not putting himself in her place.

Missteps happen in dating. And how you both react tells you a lot about your emotional readiness to handle the inevitable ups and downs that dating usually entails.

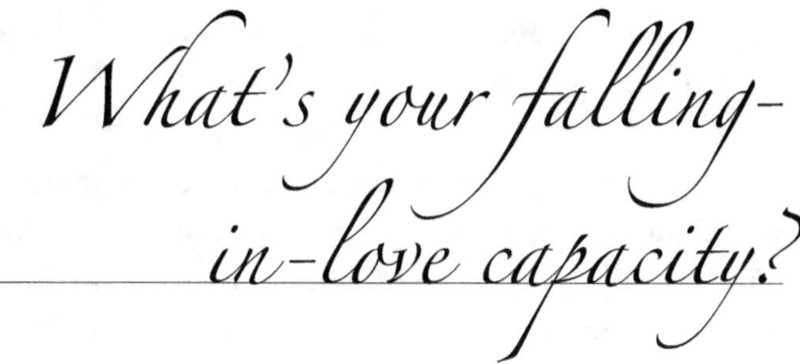

What's your falling-in-love capacity?

The other day I fell in love.

With 25 people.

I'd sent a brief pre-session questionnaire to the 25 senior managers enrolled in my 5-day seminar. Their responses were so honest, open and vulnerable that I fell in love with each of them.

Then I met them.

I fell in love again. With all of them. They were appreciative, cooperative, and supportive of me and each other. The five days flew by. We had an acknowledgment circle at the end. Tears flowed as they shared their appreciation, respect and affection toward each other. Even some of the men choked up.

It made me think of how our openness to falling in love — even non-romantic love — affects our dating, and ultimately our life.

The capacity for falling in love stems from a willingness to open your heart, to let others in. But after having fallen for someone romantically and had your heart broken, many people close their heart. They don't want to be hurt. So they live their life in fear and never experience the connection from opening your heart to another.

I understand this philosophy because I used to share it. I was cold and aloof, rarely letting anyone get close. Because when I'd let people get close, I'd be disappointed and hurt.

Disappointment still happens. Pain still happens. Heartbreak still happens.

But I can't now imagine life without an open heart. The connectedness you have with people is a feeling of no other.

I can't now imagine life without an open heart.

Some would say that is wearing your heart on your sleeve. When you "fall in love" with someone (feel fondness and affection toward someone) you barely know you are only falling for who you think they are. Which is true. But if someone shares from their core — not what they think will make them look good — it is hard to not feel connected with them.

So while I caution daters to go slow, I also think you have to open your heart. Which is not to say you go head-over-heels for someone on a first date. But just be open to connecting and protect the part that needs to know someone better before surrendering your whole heart.

If you need practice opening your heart, hang out with small children and dogs. You will quickly see how easy it is to fall in love.

Scotomas in dating

The term "scotoma" means blind spot. We all have the physical ones in our eyes, and I'd guess that we all have psychological ones, too. It means we don't see something that is right in front of us or is apparent to others.

In dating, it's easy to have a scotoma for someone we really like. We cannot see — or see but overlook — glaring signs that someone is not a good match for us. But we blissfully act as if those signs aren't there.

After a breakup it is all too clear what was present but we didn't see — or refused to acknowledge. So the question is how to be more present to traits that are ultimate deal breakers we refuse to see.

Stepping aside to view a situation objectively is not a common skill. If we are able to do this, perhaps with the aid of a friend who's willing to tell us what s/he sees, we can make a list of not only the pros of a potential mate, but the cons as well. Then we can honestly assess if we are willing to live with the trait or not.

For example, a young friend is living with her boyfriend who can be sweet and kind, but can also be unkind and selfish. He is far more immature than she, so she ends up in the mother role, angrily reminding him of the chores he leaves undone. Those who care about her see this as a terrible mismatch on many levels. She sees his foibles clearly, but ignores them when he treats her nicely. The rest of us see the totality of his behaviors and want her to see that he may change, but he may not. We ask, "Would you be happy in 5 years if nothing changed?" She would not.

When we are in the throes of new love, we often think we can live with a characteristic that we would reject if unrelated to the object of our desire. For example, many years ago "drug free" was on my list of absolute musts for a beau, but when I fell for a man who occasionally smoked pot, I told myself I was OK with it. But after we were together for a while, the pot smoking became more of a problem, as he would smoke while driving and I would get very worried when he was home late from a road trip. Had I stuck to my original requirements, I would not have become involved with someone who did drugs.

It's hard to determine what we are ignoring and what we are aware of but willing to live with. But if something is truly a scotoma, you aren't able to even see it clearly. Enlisting a friend to help you sort out what you may not be seeing takes courage and honesty, and the ability to not get mad at your friend when s/he brings up something you'd rather not see. But in the long run you are better off being fully informed rather than letting your illusions lead your heart. Eventually your illusions, just like a mirage, will dissipate and the ugly truth will cause heartache.

"No wonder he's single"

You've heard people utter this phrase about a hapless dater — or would-be dater. Perhaps you've said it yourself after a vexing encounter with a single. And of course, it can be said about either gender.

The speaker usually says it after an unpleasant interaction, or even hearing about someone's clueless behavior. I thought it myself recently after a potential suitor's second call, during which this accomplished, intelligent man was argumentative and condescending. But whenever I hear someone matter-of-factly say, "No wonder he (or she) is single," I think, "But I'm single. Just because someone is still single doesn't mean s/he is clueless, offensive, or uncouth."

I'd guess no one considers him/herself clueless, offensive, uncouth or any unflattering adjective. We justify our behavior as being appropriate based on our logic. The man I deemed argumentative probably thought he was just pointing out the flaws in my thinking. The know-it-all at Thanksgiving dinner probably thought he was just imparting his knowledge to those who didn't know what he knew — even though others shared their knowledge about the topic. The person who gets defensive and quarrelsome says she's just standing up for herself.

Can these behaviors cause someone to remain single longer than they'd like? Absolutely. Yet, I see these same behaviors in coupled people too. So did they become this way after they married? Or did their sweetie just learn to live with them? Who knows?

The fewer obnoxious behaviors you have, the easier it is to find someone who wants to be with you. So while I believe in working to reduce irritating behaviors, I also know it's impossible to eliminate them all. With focus, you can be on your best behavior for a while, but at some point you feel accepted enough to let your guard down and some of the old ways seep to the surface.

If you are brave, you can ask close friends to point out behaviors that they think might be contributing to your still being single. This takes some thick skin and the ability to hear negative feedback without getting defensive or angry. When I've had the courage to ask and fully listen, I'm reminded I still have work to do to monitor some of my off-putting behaviors.

It's easy to think that the reason you are still single is you just haven't found the right person. Yet, maybe you're doing some things that keep the right person at bay.

Have you ever asked your friends for feedback on what may be keeping you single? If so, what have you learned?

Bridge trumps relationship

A gal pal recently asked me why I thought a man would go poof after expressing great interest in a woman. The obvious answers would be:

> he was a player and said he was very interested in every woman
>
> something happened for him to lose interest (e.g., she said/did something that was off-putting; he got more interested in someone else; he got busy with work).

However, I think there is another, less commonly discussed possibility:

> He decided that if the relationship worked out, he would have to change his life patterns too much and he liked his life pretty much as it was. Even with the carrot of regular sex, it would be too much adjusting to get to that point. And besides, if a

> new relationship would be anything like his former one(s), he wouldn't be getting that regular sex for very long before he'd be putting up with an unhappy, nagging woman who wanted him to change for her to be happy.

The other day I learned that a long-time single friend had finally found a beau whom she dated exclusively for six months. However, he told her last week that he'd decided to focus on his competitive bridge (the card game) playing and therefore wouldn't have time for her. They broke up.

So this man decided that playing bridge was more of a priority than a relationship with my friend.

Keep in mind that my friend is an attractive, loving, intelligent, caring, woman, not some controlling, nagging shrew. But I have no idea if their relationship was contentious or not. For the sake of this discussion, let's assume they had an enjoyable time together, they liked hanging out together, and they liked enough of the same activities to make them compatible. But bridge wasn't something they shared. So he decided he had to choose.

We could say this was a sign he just wasn't that into her. Or it could be a sign he was clear what he wanted, and spending time in a relationship wasn't as important to him as mastering the game of bridge. I don't judge him — I think it's best to not try to lie to your partner about your priorities and make him/her think you are willing to invest time in the relationship when you aren't.

In this book we're exploring if you're ready for a relationship. Are you willing to invest time in growing the relationship? And if you know you only want something casual, do you clearly communicate that to potential suitors, so those looking for a LTR don't waste their time and their heart in you?

And if you know you have a hobby or work that you want to focus on, don't pretend you will make the time for the relationship when really you won't.

Have you ever broken up with someone when you realized you'd rather be spending time on a hobby, sport or work than with them? Or have you ever been on the receiving end of this decision? If so, how did you feel?

"I'm afraid to date"

The attractive mature woman approached me after my talk on dating after 40. She said she admired my courage to take on dating so enthusiastically, but she was afraid to start dating.

I asked what her fear was.

"I'm afraid of rejection. And I'm afraid of all the work it will take."

"Yes, there is rejection in dating. It's just part of the process unless you meet your next love on the first encounter. Some find their sweetie quickly — a friend found her fiance after dating only nine men after her divorce. Others, like me, take longer. So you have to steel yourself that there will be rejection and some men do it more respectfully than others.

"But frankly, some of the hardest rejection to deal with is when you know you must let a man know you aren't interested in having a romantic relationship. Some will take it well and others won't, no matter how nicely you put it."

"And yes, it takes time. Unless, as I said, you meet a special someone quickly. But it takes time to get to know him, ensure you have similar values, and that he's the real deal.

"But you have to weigh what you want versus the time involved. If you wanted to start playing tennis after a long absence, you'd have to put in considerable practice time. And hopefully, you'd get better and more confident the longer you practiced.

"You may start entering tournaments. And you won't win every game. You will have to deal with the disappointment of losing — just like you'll have to deal with the disappointment of being rejected in dating. But if you think of it as not really rejection, but clearing the deck for someone with whom there is mutual interest, it won't sting as much."

She nodded and smiled — and bought a book. She said she appreciated the pep talk and thought she'd now put her toe in the dating water.

If you haven't started dating again, what are you afraid of?

Rekindling a school-days sweetheart

Have you ever daydreamed about an old sweetheart from decades ago? What's he up to now? Is he single? What's he look like? If you connected, would there still be a spark?

My cousin reconnected with his high school love during their 40th reunion. They had remained close after they broke up in high school, even being in each other's first marriage wedding party! They had lost touch and hit it off again instantly at the reunion. Both were single again. She said she'd love to keep in touch, so he called the next week. The 10-hour drive didn't keep them apart. He began to woo her and a year later, they were married.

Years ago, when I was married, I got a call from a man I lived with for a year right out of college. He sounded just as stoned as he was when we were together, but he was 40 when he called, divorced and with a child. I had no interest in seeing him again.

I also heard from a college sweetheart about a decade ago. He is 8 years older than me, but when he sent his picture, I didn't recognize him. He looked so old! Solid gray hair and beard, significant weight gain. I wondered what he'd think of how his past 21-year-old love had turned out.

A man I had a crush on in high school recently looked at my profile on Match.com. He's still good looking and has a successful business. I waited a few days and since he didn't connect, I sent him a friendly, "let's catch up" email. He responded, but no overture to get together. He's looked at my profile several times since, but I won't be initiating contact again. I remember him as a good guy with an easy smile. I am curious to see if he has the same solid character he did as a teenager.

Have you considered rekindling a relationship with a high school or college sweetie? Have you ever actually met with someone you went with then? If so, what happened?

What might have been

Sometimes we find ourselves thinking about someone we would have liked to date, but it never came to be. You wonder how it might have turned out. If he's still single, you wonder if you should reconnect. Or if he's now a pal, if you should telegraph your romantic interest.

A colleague and I found ourselves single during the same time frame. We enjoyed each other's conversations, but there was never any move to go out. We shared dating stories and cheered each other on. He was always attentive and complimentary, but he never intimated that he felt other than pals.

A year ago he started dating a woman and became engaged. I was glad he'd found someone who adored him as much as he did her.

I saw him recently and updated him on my dating status. He asked how many men I've now gone out with. When I told him 105, he said he wishes he'd been in the mix.

I was surprised since I knew he was in love with his fiancée. I had no idea he would have liked to go out with me. We live several states apart, so it would have been hard to date seriously. But his comment did make me think of others I would have liked to have dated, to see if it would have worked out.

Do you daydream about men who got away? That you would have liked to have dated but it didn't happen for whatever reason? If so, have you made contact to see what might evolve?

What part of you is your date calling forth?

We like our friends, in part, because of who we are when we are with them. We feel we can relax and be our best self.

Unlike how we feel when we are around people who we find difficult, obnoxious or off-putting. Part of why we don't like being around those folks is because we don't like how we feel around them.

Another way to say this is: around our friends, our true self is called forth. We feel good, comfortable, relaxed.

When we are exploring a new relationship, it's important to be aware of what part of you is called forth. Do you feel comfortable, safe and relaxed? Do you feel kind, accepting and generous? Or do you get defensive, angry, or competitive?

Most people aren't conscious of what is being called forth; they just decide they like someone or not. They don't realize that part of why they like or dislike a person is based on how they feel around them and what part of them is brought out.

I was discussing a mutual colleague with a pal. I said, "I don't like how I'm triggered to be when I'm around him." Yes, you can consciously choose how you behave around others. But the people who elicit the strongest negative reactions are those who trigger something deep within us — some old hurt. We find ourselves reacting before giving any thought to the situation.

So when starting to get to know a potential romantic partner, be mindful of what part of you is being called forth. If you feel wonderful and rarely confused or upset, keep seeing him. But if you find yourself regularly feeling defensive, hurt or angry, move on.

However, know that some relationship counselors suggest that if you are able to hang out in the negative emotion, you can work to heal that old hurt so it no longer has any power over you. But this is an advanced skill that is hard to master. I have, on occasion, realized that the negative emotion a beau evoked was an opportunity to look at the underlying old hurt and heal it. By healing it, one is no longer susceptible to the triggers, so isn't bothered by the behaviors that called forth the disappointment.

After a date, ask yourself, "How did I feel? Was my best self called forth? Was I kind, generous, interested a good listener? Or did I find myself getting irritated with him over little things?" If the later, best to move on, unless there are other overriding characteristics that will make it worth your while to notice and examine the negative triggers.

Have you noticed how you feel after a date and identified what part of you was called forth? What did you notice and what did you do about it?

Resources

Make sure to download your free eBook Attract Your Next Great Mate: Dating Advice From Top Relationship Experts *at www.DatingGoddess.com/freebie*

Afterword

At the time of this writing, I have not yet found my true King Charming. I continue my search with verve. I've become more discerning about what I want and don't want. I've met some wonderful men pals — my treasures — who continue to be in touch.

I wish you much luck in your adventure. It will be fun and frustrating, exhilarating and exasperating, and sexy or sexless. So much depends on you, your approach and your attitude. My books are designed to help you enjoy as much as possible and ward off unpleasantness. But nearly all adventures have wonderful highs as well as a few lows. If you know that going in and arm yourself with information on what to expect, you'll have more of the positives and fewer of the negatives.

Please drop by www.DatingGoddess.com and join in the discussion and report on your experiences.

Dating Goddess

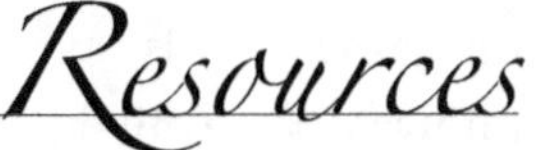

Resources

Go to www.datinggoddess.com to access a variety of useful resources. We work to suggest resources we think have value.

Dating and relationship book reviews

These reviews will save you time and money as I've given you my take on specific books, CDs and more. Some are worth your effort to buy and read or listen to them — some are not. We're always adding new book reviews, so check frequently. We'll also notify our mailing list when new resources are added.

Dating site links

There are a lot of dating sites on the Internet. I've listed the ones I think are worth investigating.

Dating products and tools

Dating can be daunting. We're continually looking at

ways to make it easier and more fun. We'll provide info on games, tools, even date-wear that will help others know you're available, or help you get to know potential suitors better.

Dating and relationship advice sites

Advice "experts" abound on the Internet as anyone can self-proclaim themseves as expert — even if they haven't dated in 30 years and never in midlife. I've worked to find experts who's advice I generally think is solid.

Midlife recources

We'll feature Web sites, books, events and other resources we think might interest you.

Newly discovered resources

I'll add other resources as we discover them. Subscribe to our mailing list to get the scoop as soon as we find them —go to www.DatingGoddess.com to register. Don't worry, we won't sell or give your email to anyone.

Acknowledgments

Let me start by acknowledging the 91 men who helped trigger the lessons contained in this book. Some prompted several! They remain nameless here to protect their identity, although most would recognize references to them. Plus the thousands more whose winks, emails and calls didn't result in a date, but helped me learn the dating game. And all those men who I emailed who never responded — such a blessing to have them weed themselves out.

I acknowledge the 91 men who triggered my lessons

I'd like to thank my Seven Sisters mastermind group for the tremendous brainstorming, noodling, strategizing and encouragement. I wouldn't have begun this project without the prodding of Val Cade, Chris Clarke-Epstein, Mariah Burton Nelson, Sue Dyer, Sam Horn and Marilynn Mobley.

Thank you to my good friends who've listened to my dating stories ad nauseam, and whose support and wisdom are embedded in this text. Ed Betts, Ken Braly, Bruce Daley, Tom Drews, Elaine Floyd, Paulette Ensign, Scott Friedman, Craig Harrison, Mary Jansen, Tom Johnson, Sandy Jones, Mary Kilkenny, Ellie Klevins, Patrick Lynch, Mary Marcdante, Barbara McNichol, Ann Peterson, Anthony Ramsey, Caterina Rando, Kristy Rogers, Jana Stanfield, Holly Stiel, Terry Tepliz, and George Walther, thank you.

The Adventures in Delicious Dating After 40 series

The Adventures in Delicious Dating After 40 series is designed to help you understand your own midlife dating journey. It is not a road map, as we all take different routes. It is a guide to help you understand yourself, midlife men, and the dating process. Hopefully, you'll not only learn from the lessons and insights shared in this series, but you'll examine how they apply — or don't — to your own dating adventure.

You'll get the scoop on what you need to know, what's changed since you last dated, and how to navigate inevitable bumps in the road.

Following is an overview of each book in the series and a sampling of some of the chapter titles. All are detailed at www.DatingGoddess.com.

Date or Wait: Are You Ready for Mr. Great?

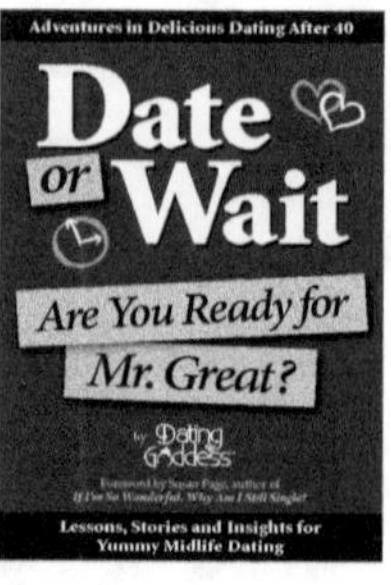

Are you ready for a special man in your life? You have a great life. But you know you'd like a special man to share it. You think you're ready to date, but you haven't done it in a while.

What should you consider before you actually start dating full bore? Even if you've reentered the dating world, this will give you a foundation of attitude and philosophy to make your adventure more fulfilling.

Sample chapters

- From hurt to flirt
- Dating is like Baskin-Robbins
- You've got to kiss a lot of…princes!
- What's your definition of dating success?
- Are you open to receiving?
- Dating: A self-designed personal-growth workshop
- Hands-on dating research
- Being present to the presents
- Being aggressively single
- Approaching dating like a buffet
- Is Brad Pitt ruining your love life?
- Treasures can come in dented packages

Assessing Your Assets: Why You're A Great Catch

You have many wonderful qualities. But it's easy to focus on one's flaws — at least what seem like flaws to you. However, to the right man your imperfections are endearing, attractive and lovable. You have to be clear what you offer a man who will find you enchanting.

Assessing Your Assets helps you look at what you bring to a new relationship. It will help you see your good points so you'll approach dating with more confidence.

Sample chapters

- Don't think you are damaged goods
- You are (probably) more attractive than you think!
- They aren't called "hate handles"
- Are you a good man picker?
- What are your deal breakers?
- Are you arguing your limitations?
- Turn your liabilities into assets
- The strong vs. nice woman debate
- Is your sense of humor stunting your dating?
- Why are we drawn to bad boys?
- The zest test

In Search of King Charming: Who Do I Want to Share My Throne?

You are no longer looking for "Prince" Charming because you are a queen. You want someone who is at your level, not groveling at your feet. You want a king — someone who's your equal and with whom you can rule the throne together!

This book focuses on helping you better define what you want beyond tall, dark and handsome! You'll consider characteristics you might not have thought of before. You'll look at what you want now.

Sample chapters

- Building your Franken-boyfriend
- What's your "perfect boyfriend's" job description?
- A man to go with your wardrobe
- In search of the elusive good kisser
- When you're clear on what you want, it appears
- Are you dating the same guy in different bodies?
- Does he fit in your world?
- What's your kissing quotient?
- Is your guy's loving muscle strong?
- Do you both have the same dating rhythm?
- Does your date nourish your mind?

Embracing Midlife Men: *Insights Into Curious Behaviors*

Do you sometimes scratch your head after interacting with a midlife man, wondering, "What could he possibly be thinking?" Especially if it's before, during or after a date with a man who presumably wants to impress you!

This book focuses on better understanding midlife men's behaviors. When you grasp what's going on in his head it's much easier to embrace him. Men are wondrous creatures, so we need to understand them better and love them for who they are.

Sample chapters

- Men are like shoes
- Why men disappear when it gets serious
- Chivalry isn't dead —but it seems to be hibernating
- Do men want feisty women?
- Midlife men have forgotten how to date
- Are you getting prime time from your man?
- When a man tells you what he paid for things
- Does he treat you like his ex?
- Has Greg Behrendt done women a disservice?
- Tales of woo

Dipping Your Toe in the Dating Pool: Dive In Without Belly Flopping

You've decided you are ready — you want to start dating. Maybe you've already had a few coffee dates with several men. You want to be as successful as possible on your dating adventure.

This book focuses on getting started on your dating adventures. We cover what you need to know as you begin your journey.

Sample chapters

- Do you have the right datewear?
- Dating with integrity
- Building your rejection muscle
- When "be yourself" is questionable advice
- Faux beaus and practice dating
- Are you making bad decisions out of loneliness?
- Being "in wonder" about your date's behavior
- When do you feel most vulnerable in dating?
- Are you out of his league — or he yours?
- Why listening is so seductive

Winning at the Online Dating Game: Stack the Deck in Your Favor

Internet dating can be frustrating or fruitful. It will be much less exasperating if you know how to read and weed out men's profiles that aren't appropriate for you. And you'll have a steady stream of potential suitors if you know how to write a compelling profile for yourself.

This book focuses on the ins and outs of online dating. How to play the game, which has it's own rules and language. If you don't understand how online dating works, you'll waste a lot of time connecting with men who are not a possible fit for you.

Sample chapters

- Shopping for men
- Safe online dating
- Is 21st Century dating unnatural?
- What do men look at in your profile?
- Euphemisms uncovered
- Are you describing yourself compellingly?
- No, I will not be dating your Harley
- Playing the online dating game
- Scantily clothed pictures
- Online dating time equivalent to dog years

Check Him Out Before Going Out: Avoiding Dud Dates

Under the cloak of the anonymity that email and the phone provides, men often reveal more than they intend. If you ask the right questions you can find out a lot about his values and view of the world after just an interaction or two.

This book focuses on what you need to ask before agreeing to even a coffee date. You need to vet the men who email and call you to ensure you're not likely to waste your time with men who clearly aren't a match.

Sample chapters

- Becoming smitten with the fantasy
- Can Google help — or hinder — your dating life?
- Qualify your potential dates before meeting
- The art of consideration
- Anticipating a big date is like awaiting Santa
- Being seduced by what he is over who he is
- Are you his spare?
- My boyfriend, whom I haven't met
- When canceling is the right thing to do
- Politics, religion and sex — oh my!

First-Rate First Dates: Increasing the Chances of a Second Date

You can tell a lot about someone within the first 30 minutes. What does he talk about? Does he ask you questions? If so, what does he want to know about you? What do you need to know about him? How does he treat you? How does he treat those around you?

This book focuses on what goes on during the first date. How do you determine if you want a second date? What you can do to increase the likelihood your date will ask you for a second? That is if you want a repeat!

Sample chapters

- Start with coffee
- How do you greet him?
- When it clicks, throw out some of your criteria
- Tracking your date's score
- Clues a guy is just looking for a booty call
- 12 signs he won't be asking for a second date
- First-date red flags that this guy isn't for you
- Honesty is not always the best policy
- Chemistry, or does he make my toes curl?
- Women's first-date blunders

Real Deal or Faux Beau: Should You Keep Seeing Him?

You've begun to go out with a man you like. How do you decide if you should continue seeing him, or if you should release him because he's not The One?

This book focuses on second dates and beyond. During the dating process you are both assessing if you want to keep seeing each other. This book helps you determine what questions you need to ask yourself.

Sample chapters

- Deciding to see him again or not
- What's your date's Delight/Disappointment Scale score?
- Broaching tough conversations
- "I want to respect me in the morning"
- Does he invite you to his place?
- Are you stingy in dating?
- When his hand is on your knee too soon
- Easy way to ask hard questions
- Rose-colored glasses obscure red flags
- If his stories don't add up, subtract yourself

Multidating Responsibly: ***Play the Field Without Being A Player***

Playing the field is frowned on in some circles. There are definitely appropriate and inappropriate ways to date several men simultaneously.

This book focuses on how to date around responsibly and with integrity without leading men on. If you do it with honesty, you can date several people at once until you're both ready to focus only on each other.

Sample chapters

- "Pimpin'" — Dating multiple guys
- Multi-dating pros and cons
- Your Date-A-Base — tracking multiple suitors
- "Hot bunking" your beaus
- Are you a "Let's Make a Deal" type of dater?
- Assume there are other women
- Dating's revolving door
- How long do you hedge your bet?
- Beware of multi-tasking when multi-dating
- Back burner beaus
- The boyfriend phone

Moving On Gracefully: Break Up Without Heartache

"Breaking up" sounds so high school, doesn't it? But part of the dating process is saying something when one of you decides not to date the other anymore. Going "poof" is not a mature or respectful option in midlife.

This book focuses on surviving a breakup, whether you initiate it or not. Either way, it's never easy to break up if you have developed any fondness toward the other.

Sample chapters

- Hello — goodbye: How to say no thanks after meeting
- Releasing back into the dating pool
- 50 ways to leave your lover? 4 ways not to leave your suitor
- Breaking up is hard to do — right
- Why men go "poof"
- How to trump being dumped
- When breaking up is a "Get Out of Jail Free" card
- How to detect the end is near
- Failed relationships' blessings
- He's broken up with you — he just didn't tell you
- Rejection is protection

From Fear to Frolic: Get Naked Without Getting Embarrassed

This book focuses on what you need to consider and know before getting physically intimate with a man you're dating. This is nerve-wracking to many midlife women. This book will prepare you.

Sample chapters

- Sleepover do's and don'ts
- Does he want in your life — or just in your bedroom?
- Getting naked with him the first time
- An excuse to seduce or how important is bed-room bliss?
- What to ask yourself before getting naked with him
- Are you and your guy on the same sexual time line?
- Sharing your sexual owner's manual with him
- What women need from a man before having sex
- Why too-soon midlife sex is like non-fat food
- How dating sex is like waffles
- Too-soon seduction: "I'm special, but not THAT special"

Ironing Out Dating Wrinkles: Work Through Challenges Without Getting Steamed

Nearly all relationships have some ups and downs. Part of getting to know someone is knowing how they work through relationship misunderstandings.

This book focuses on how to work through the inevitable hiccups that happen when you are getting to know each other. If you can both deal with challenges, the bond deepens and you find yourself smitten.

Sample chapters

- When your guy vexes you, ask what your highest self would do
- The first fight
- You want boo; he wants boo-ty
- Where's the line between getting your needs met and being selfish?
- Expressing your upset with your guy
- Is his toothbrush in your cabinet too soon?
- Do you love how he loves you?
- Is he collecting data on how to make you happy?
- Be careful of being smitten
- Exclusivity: How and when to broach it
- The 60-day relationship review

www.ingramcontent.com/pod-product-compliance
Lightning Source LLC
Chambersburg PA
CBHW051555030726
47592CB00001B/308